George O'Brien was brough
ford. He left Ireland in 1965
years, and was educated at F
his BA and Ph.D. at the U
lectured in English from 1976 to 1980. He was then appointed
assistant professor of English at Vassar College in New York
and in 1984 took up a similar position at Georgetown
University, Washington, DC. He was awarded a Hennessy/
New Irish Writing Prize in 1973 for his short stories, and *The
Village of Longing* won the 1988 Irish Book Awards Silver
Medal for Literature.

The
Village
of
Longing

GEORGE O'BRIEN

THE
BLACKSTAFF
PRESS

BELFAST

First published in 1987 by
The Lilliput Press
and simultaneously by
The Sixth Chamber Press
with a limited edition of twenty-five copies

First published with *Dancehall Days* (as one volume)
in hardback in 1989 by
Viking
Published in paperback in 1990 by
Penguin Books

This Blackstaff Press edition of *The Village of Longing*
is a photolithographic facsimile of the 1987 Lilliput edition
printed by Richard Clay (The Chaucer Press) Limited, Bungay, Suffolk

This edition of *The Village of Longing* published in 1993 by
The Blackstaff Press Limited
3 Galway Park, Dundonald, Belfast BT16 0AN, Northern Ireland
with the assistance of
The Arts Council of Northern Ireland

Printed by The Guernsey Press Company Limited

A catalogue record for this book
is available from the British Library

ISBN 0-85640-519-1

for Ben and Nick: 'two fine boys'

CONTENTS

I

MY THREE PARENTS

1

It's teatime.

Chrissy, my aunt, is slicing a cottage loaf with a crackle and spray of delicious black crust. She's humming a song-hit, 'Shrimp Boats', or maybe the new Rosemary Clooney, 'Mambo Italiano'. Her brother George - Georgie, we call him, or often, 'Geo': 'jaw' – will be in from work soon. The meaty tang of his dinner sits in the steamy kitchen air, heavy male aroma (Geo is all smells: paint, putty, sawdust, Brylcreem, booze). At the sink, Mam, my grandmother, is in the posture I will see her in forever, crouched slightly, head bent over some chore, wisps of grey hair bothersomely hanging around her hard, handsome face.

I wonder if she's going to Lyons's tonight.

For a year or more when I was nine or ten (in the pages that follow I'm seven going on twelve) she regularly visited Bid and Willy Lyons after the chapel. The chapel came first, needless to say. Mam wouldn't dream of missing morning mass at the convent or of closing the day without 'paying a visit'. Off with the apron and dull grey skirt, on with the cloche hat and kid gloves, and away with her, hail, rain or snow, her crisp gait and erect bearing announcing to Lismore at large the uprightness and quiet implacability of her faith.

Handily enough, the Lyonses lived in Chapel Street, just opposite the chapel's tall, white, ever-open gates. Too near, in my view. Wouldn't the Angelus, funeral and mass bells deafen them? (Joe Kelly, who lived next door, *was* deaf.) And then, living so close, they wouldn't be able to feel what I thought was the best part of going. Being just-on-the-verge-of, feeling just-about-to-be. Voluptuous anticipation: a feeling finer than any offered by the services, which for all their otherworldly overtures, were predictable down to the congregation's last cough.

Chapel Street was dull and poor and quiet. I didn't care for it. It looked lonesome. Few youngsters lived there. Mam loved Chapel Street, though. Proud as she was to have married into Main Street and a fine, detached house like Swiss Cottage, she never denied the cabin she was born in. From her loyalty to the street she could even speak with pride about Tim Healy, the noted turncoat of Parnell's time, though she never knew him and despised his unprincipled politicking. But his father ran the Union (poor-house), as the hospital was called in her young day, and it pleased her to think that through that connection, less than ideal though it was, Chapel Street silently, surreptitiously but nevertheless indelibly, was borne beyond itself into the world of affairs and men. Mam was an embodiment of the extraordinary powers and accuracy of the appeal in the words *sinn féin*: ourselves. And it was her fierce, pleasure-giving fidelity that brought her to Lyons's: Willy was one of the old stock.

The same could not be said for Bid. No-neck Bid was coarse, outspoken, ill-mannered and unpredictable. She was not altogether 'no class', a term Mam used to pigeon-hole and at the same time explain boorish uppityness. But she'd 'read the riot act', 'leaving nothing unsaid' to an antagonist, and 'live where another would die' (of embarrassment) – delighted in doing so. Mam detested such letting of bad blood, and Bid's revelling in it. She was a suppressor, and desired others to be the same.

But Mam had an excuse for Bid and her red-faced choler. She wasn't from Lismore, a place which was, for Mam, a moral Switzerland, where decorum had been the order of the day since the Blackwater River first carved out its somnolent, deeply wooded valley and offered a crossing-point for the town to settle on. Bid wasn't even from County Waterford, but from the river valley on the far side of the Knockmealdowns (our mountains), from the garrison town of Clonmel, or rather from Irishtown, whence she'd arrived with her raucous ways to serve in the scullery of one of the numerous big houses that made our valley a colony more enduring and elaborate than anything merely military.

And now, here was this pugilist married to someone who

was, Mam assured me solemnly, 'every inch a gentleman'. He certainly looked the part. Being retired, Willy never wore work-clothes. I knew few men of any age of whom that was true, and hardly any that the family was on first-name terms with. Willy carried a walking-cane whose varnish glistened – not for him the grimy ash-plant of local old-stagers like Marsh Reagan and Pike Parker, Willy's childhood playmates, who unlike him had not retired but were too old and sore to work. Another thing that impressed me: unlike those contemporaries of his, Willy didn't have a nickname, which placed him in the exclusive 'Mister' category, making him virtually a Protestant. And, finally, for me the finishing touch, he had a moustache, that ribbon of venerability which all the most imposing adults wore. My late grandfather (Mam's gifted George) had one. The toffs who came to the door with jobs for him and Georgie – Colonel Foster, I remember, and Captain Jameson – wore them, thin silvery ones against plump, pink complexions: cirrus at sunset. (Priests never had them, but we never regarded them as rich, grand or special. They were just poor boys, raised far away from town and comfort, peasants doing the best they could without presence or polish.)

Despite Willy's impressive appearance, however, not quite every inch of him, I thought, lived up to Mam's assurance. The eyes were wrong. Bloodshot, watery, slightly exophthalmic, they gave him a wounded, fugitive, startled look. I watched him pass by on the other side and out the convent road on his daily constitutional, shuffling slowly, breathing heavily, his look exerting a fearful fascination on me. What gave him that?

'He', said Mam, 'was a high-up in the Post Office over in England; the right-hand man of some big-bug. Worked his way up. One of the cleverest boys ever to leave the town of Lismore.'

Mam's lips just smacked, she so relished the authority with which she made such statements, and the classiness of the achievement.

'How did he work himself up?' I wanted to know.

'He wanted to get on,' said Mam, 'so he studied by night, and passed his exams, and sure enough in no time he was sitting pretty in London West Central.'

London West Central, studying by night, getting on: enchanting universe of potential! That picture in Georgie's old geography book: 'Cheapside', tall loaf-like buildings, ungainly trolley buses, and the caption 'Centre of World Commerce'. Post-office exams! The idea of them settled in my mind as an archetype of obscurity, hardship and delicious challenge.

And Willy had triumphed. He was of the same calibre as my Uncle Frank who got a university scholarship, was a Bachelor of Civil Engineering, and now was building a railway in Tanganyika. On Sundays he drove forty miles through dust to hear mass from a German priest. Or Kathleen, B.Sc. (another scholarship, this time the prestigious Earl of Cork, no less). She was making 'planes in Bristol. But did their going mean they might come back like Willy, broken somehow, wheezing, needing strange partners to see them through? It could. Look at my father. He went away to be a teacher and then his only love, my mother, died. Or was that different?

Perhaps Willy himself could have told me. As things turned out I had plenty of opportunities to ask him. But I never did. I never asked him anything. To the end he remained for me an icon of the world's inscrutable ways.

The questions Mam had answered about Willy were prompted by my seeing him out walking. The period of her visits, and then mine, was later, when he became bedridden.

I can't remember now exactly how my visits started. Maybe I was going through one of my bouts of self-imposed piety and felt that practising one of the corporal works of mercy – visiting the sick – would be a suitable expression of my pretensions. Or it might have been that, under the task of the Passionist father who came to conduct the Easter observances (my visits began, I remember, in silky-aired April), I thought I should volunteer for a spell of self-denial, and thereby improve myself even beyond their ambitions for me. At any rate, I'm sure I made my offer freely (no prompting from Mam; she dealt in righteousness, not piety), and judging by the kind of offer it was – I would read to the invalid – showing off figured prominently in my motivation.

Not that my offer was all ego. When I was sick, being read to was really the best bit, better even than warm lemonade. I remember Chrissy sitting in her overcoat in my freezing bedroom rattling off reams of *Treasure Island* to me, while I snuggled up to the hot-water bottle, drugged to the eyeballs by the pleasures of weakness.

I wasn't all altruism, either, of course. The thought of sampling Bid's temperament at first hand was alarming. Mightn't she eat me if I did something wrong (and childhood, I'd learned, was a phase of inevitable wrong-doing)? And I didn't know how I would handle coming face-to-face with Willy, or how he would take to me (would I cry if he wheeled his baleful eyes towards me? – I always cried at home when I couldn't understand). But then there was the attraction of going into someone else's house. I loved other people's strange air and the different ways they found to arrange familiarity. I loved their quirky trinkets, their mottoes in pokerwork, the placid grey of their ghostly old photos.

Willy's room was at the back of the house, downstairs, at the end of the cramped hall, overlooking the deranged and fruit-less garden, where Bid's cats prowled. Bid's mother was foster-mother to at least half a dozen menacing toms, and took pride in reciting their complex genealogy: 'This fella's that fella's uncle. Go on ya vagabond!' her endearment accompanied by strong blows to the place lately vacated by the mother-wise moggy. 'The óinseach,' said Mam harshly, back home. 'Fit her better to air the house.' True, the house stank of cat, and the stench mingled with the smells of Willy's room, sweat, pee, and vinegary medical essences arrayed in amber bottles and ruby phials on the nightstand. Mam always let the window down a crack before I began the evening's read. But I felt it was inappropriate to expect Bid to keep house, now that I'd seen close up the spiky ginger of her manner and heard her harangue the neighbourhood in the language of green-eyed suspicion. Out prowling around, looking for fight and staking out territory, is what she really should have been doing, it seemed, leaving steadfast, concentrated Mam to abide the alternative life of the sick-room.

Besides smells, Willy's room was smothered in holiness. An *Infant de Prague* stood pertly to attention in his tight-fitting tunic on a ledge by the door, the cross-topped globe in his hand no more a burden to him than a ping-pong ball. The holy-water font hanging from a nail by the light switch was a memento of Lourdes. The figure on the heavily varnished crucifix at the head of the bed was as naked and as abject as a scavenged bone. And from the wall at the foot of the bed a fully

7

bearded Saviour in a purplish frock looked down, his bosom wounded. This was the Sacred Heart. He wore a slightly anxious look, profferring his velvety valentine with its accessories of flame and fletched arrows. Willy stared at him a lot, inert in the big brass bed, forbidden to move, all his energy consumed by breathing.

My reading started with *Seven Years in Tibet* by Heinrích Harrer, a choice of which I was extremely proud, since it was a grown-up's book in every sense of the word. It was a far cry from Enid Blyton, Patricia Lynch and the Hardy Boys, for one thing. That's not to say that Noddy, Longears the turf-cutter's donkey and Franklin W. Dixon were by then beneath me. But they were only stories, and *Seven Years in Tibet* was true, and had photos to prove it. The stony places and flattened faces fascinated me. The shaggy yaks, the prayer-wheels, the windy emptiness of the Roof of the World, the tea with butter, the bright saffron of the monks' habits. . . . The idea of being on the same planet as such strangeness was as powerful to me as something from the Gospels.

As well as that, and also very pleasing, this book was our own, not borrowed from the library, like most of what was read in Swiss Cottage. Someone, possibly my Aunt Elizabeth (a nurse in England), thought we could do with belonging to a book-club, so World Books plied us with its choices, mainly stories for big people by authors with remote, unlikely names – Rumer Godden, Nevil Shute, Pamela Frankau. From time to time something really foreign turned up, like the Harrer (Lorenz's *King Solomon's Ring* was another), which meant that I too could join in, savour at home the schoolroom scents of new paper and fresh ink, hear the crackle of gummy joints as the spine stretched, admire the livery – forthcoming titles surrounded by signs of the zodiac on the back of the dust-wrapper and the vivid splash of colour on the front, butter yellow for *Seven Years in Tibet*.

I remember the jacket better than I do the contents. In those days, and for too many years after, I read for speed, not thought. My only substantial recollection is of how the Dalai Lama came to be, of how a child of parents humbler than Christ's in an out-of-the-way place like one of the mountainy townlands around Lismore, was sanctified by being found and properly identified. That part stuck only because it aggravated my own incurable desire to be claimed and elevated, meaning not that I wanted to rule the world but that I ached to go to Dublin and live with my father.

The reading consisted of rattling on regardless. I'd arrive about half-seven and charge ahead with hardly a civil word to the invalid, my headlong canter competing with the chatter of the women in the kitchen. At about half-nine I'd stop because of failing light (Bid didn't think the act of mercy worth using electricity for). My idea was to perform, not to embody, to let the words fall where they may and be applauded afterwards. I was all spray and no tide. As far as I knew, that was the way to be. Depth was not something I was used to. Slogan, joke, curse, song, proverb: these were our parts of speech. The reply churlish, the counter-check quarrelsome. But I never knew anyone who could explain, or appear calmly and without defence to think about something. Priests, teachers and adults just told whoever was in earshot what to do and what not – all assertion, no questioning.

Passive Willy was not the one to challenge my behaviour. Played-out as he was, if anything he merely confirmed it as appropriate, the rubble of pebbles (which was as much as my verbalizing amounted to) making a fragile causeway to something broader than the bed. And I was delighted to prate away: I never got restless or bored or tired of the sound of my own voice. Willy sang dumb throughout, offering only a few words in parting to Mam when the session ended. But I didn't need him to say anything: I firmly believed that he had to be enjoying it because I was doing it for him.

I demolished *Seven Years in Tibet* in next to no time, and with hardly a pause for breath jumped to the next selection, *Annapurna*. Excellent choice, I thought smugly: another true story, another World Book, another grand jacket, this time in piercing ice-blue. But *Annapurna* was my downfall. I liked the bit about the man losing some of his toes due to cold: that made the flesh tingle pleasurably. But I had to labour to get that far, had to barge and hack my way as best I could through stretches infested with 'rendezvous', 'bivouac' and the dreaded 'cwm'. I cursed the English language for having kept such barbed tripwires to itself until now. I sat in the upright kitchen chair, sweating and slurring and palpably losing face.

But *Annapurna* is memorable for another reason too. It   9 brought about the only conversation that's remained with me from those evenings. Willy's breath was in such short supply that it may have been our only one, and besides, part of his novelty was his total lack of interest in me and my child's life, an indifference unique among adults of my acquaintance. So, I was most surprised when, quite out of the blue, Willy interrupted my assault to ask what part of the world were we in now.

'The Himalayas,' said I.

He seemed to brighten. 'Isn't that India?' he said.

I told him it was.

'Tell me,' he said, 'what about –' And he rolled off a list of names I'd never heard of, Baluchistan, Gujarat, Rajaishan. . . . I was struck dumb. Clueless. 'Rendezvous' and its fellow-travellers were nursery slopes compared to these! All I could think was that I'd never come across any of these names in my stamp-album. If Stanley Gibbons & Co. had no place for them . . .

'They're gone,' I said.

'Ayeh,' said Willy, with a wondering sigh. 'Gone?'

'There's only India now,' I said, with bold finality. 'And Pakistan.'

'Pakistan,' Willy repeated, as though he caught an echo of something in the name. Then he fell silent again.

'Yes,' I said, confident now (philately hadn't let me down: I'd been told it would be good for me). 'The places you're talking about all are gone.' I dare say I even knew what 'gone' meant. It never occurred to me what Willy's echo might have contained, what exotic telegraphy might have passed along those fading nerves, what inkling of an old, deep-burning yen. I never thought. I returned to *Annapurna*, all the better equipped to tackle it with smugness my fuel.

As things turned out, however, I didn't get much further with it or any other book. Summer grew strong and I wanted to be out in the air. Then, as happened every school holiday, either my father came down or I went up to Dublin – either this dream personage (tolerant, unfussy, playful) appeared and I forsook everyone and everything to devote all my time to him, or I was transported to a more vital realm where, seeing myself as a mixture of sophisticated princeling and rehabilitated prodigal, I believed I belonged only to find, year after year, the belief turn to hunger.

At any rate I was not to return to Lyons's for in the autumn Willy was removed to Dungarvan (where the nearest full-scale hospital was).

We were in the kitchen when Chrissy brought in the news, adding in the plain, clipped tone she used to convey a particularly notable item of gossip, 'Bid ran after the ambulance going "Willy – Willy – Willy".'

'The blasted foolah,' said Mam harshly. The response was predictable. Mam detested displays. When her man went she just sat in the parlour, hour after hour, staring at air, mute as a severed limb. But why was her tone like a lash?

Maybe it was easier to attack Bid instead of to think about Willy. After all, someone his age only went to hospital to die. And there he was now, stretched out as a case, enfolded in linen premonitorily starched. The bright boy. The gentleman. Her oldest man-friend. Maybe she was trying not to be reminded of her dead George, and of how Willy had reminded her that she'd been young. Springtime evening strolls down the Green Road, skating on the flooded 'inch' (the riverbank) in hardy January, strong arms to be held in dancing the lancers and schottische to a crisp military band in the Courthouse.

Maybe. If Willy's going caused any pang or hankering in Mam, she didn't show it. All that followed her remark was a minute or two of stillness before the cups were cleared. I fell back on my own thoughts: the room, the words, the summer air freighted with the hoarse breath of dying.

2

Impressed as I was with myself for taking on all that reading and amassing all that merit, the evenings I really lived for were those when Mam went to Lyons's alone, and I had what I most wanted in the world, Chrissy's undivided attention.

Mam was principle and steadfastness, duty and its long-suffering sister, self-denial. Chrissy was pure enjoyment.

Mam was the long haul. Chrissy was the moment; Mam the speech from the dock, Chris the tune on the wireless. We had fine times, we two – music, warm fires and gusts of giggling.

We wrote stories, or maybe it was just one long story that we made several attempts at. It was about Pat and Mag, two tramps, on their way to Drumshambo. Pat and Mag were real people, real tramps, who turned up in Lismore every so often. Pat had the cut of an ex-soldier about him. He was fairly tall, wiry, had close-cropped foxy hair and carried himself with a brash stride. Also, he had a moustache. Mag, though, was a dolt. Shapeless, moon-faced, with a shuffle not a walk, she looked totally downtrodden. She wore a man's gaberdine coat a couple of sizes too big for her, buttoned from neck to calf. She always went in her hair, hail, rain or snow. And winter or summer she only wore wellingtons.

These really were the lowest of the low, much worse than tinkers, not that we regarded tinkers favourably – far from it, begging was treated most uncharitably in our house, being thought of as, quite simply, a blatant deficiency in self-respect. But tinkers were something. Their shawls, ponies, caravans, squads of children, added up to a style and an identity. They even had names – Hogan, Connors, Sheridan. They flung their washing gaily on the bushes to dry. None of this was true of Pat and Mag.

'Where do they sleep, Chris?' I remember asking.

'Out the road under a hedge,' she replied, off-hand, matter-of-fact, and for a minute I thrilled to my own good fortune.

They never did get to Drumshambo. Just as well for them. Once there I'd have had to abandon them, anyway, since I knew nothing whatever about that town, only that it was far, far away in a part of the country I had no connection with and, therefore, not the slightest interest in. I only thought of it for the story because it sounded funny. (It made me feel superior not to be from funny-sounding places such as Ballydehob, Knocknagopall, Ringaskiddy and, the village nearest Lismore, Cappoquin.)

The reason Pat and Mag never got anywhere was not because I, for all my tender years, subconsciously appreciated that their tramps' existence should exemplify an inherent, Beckettian incompleteness, but because I wanted to play the drums. Writing was a chore, and gave very poor returns for the amount of time spent on it. All too few of the moments, in the moment-by-moment activity of writing, were ink-filled. Rather than passing time, writing seemed an exposure to the possibility of being overrun by time. Kneeling on a chair at the Swiss Cottage kitchen table, bent over a copy-book, crude, wooden-shafted pen poised, pleading, 'What'll I put now, Chrissy?' – that's how I think of writing, a desire not to be stuck.

Drumming had no such problems, especially when I had such a receptive instrument as an oil-stove and such pliable sticks as the axles of a defunct toy truck complete with rubberized wheels. With the amount of bounce they gave I could roll and flim-flam away to my heart's content, Chrissy's light soprano wafting gamely above the uproar.

I never thought of drumming as keeping time – any fool could do that – but as embellishing the time signature to the point of sublimation, if not downright suppression. The beat could be carried by the merest tapping of a foot. What I wanted was the spray and rumble that filled the intervals. I kicked the side of the heater just as a metronomical matter of course, not because I thought there was a chance of losing my footing.

My barrage caused problems, though. The heater – a Rippingille Fyreside, a much classier item than the upright Valor favoured by most families – was newfangled and temperamental. It operated by allowing the paraffin to drip slowly into the wick, and needed a totally flat surface in order to behave properly, as an aid to which it had adjustable legs. Needless to say, my time-keeping resulted in substantial maladjustment, which let in poor Fyreside for more beating, this time from Mam, who hammered it with the side of her fist and muttered bitter criticism of Chrissy, whom she suspected of having been soft-talked into recommending the paraffin prima donna by Joe Wall of the Co-op. Beating objects could improve their behaviour: Georgie often went a few rounds with the radio and sobered it of static. People were not beaten (only once did Mam hit me a clatter across the face); frosty looks and icy silences invariably proved to be lash enough.

Instead of an oil-heater I should have had a Trinidadian oil-drum, but as things stood I rattled away, as happy as Larry. I favoured martial airs: two half-Emperor rolls to start, and I

13

was off, my mind a gaudy parade. And sometimes for good measure I twirled my axles in the air (once a wheel flew off and landed – *plop!* – in Chrissy's tea: such laughs . . .), as I'd seen the side-drummers of the Mellary pipers do. Easy for them, though; their sticks had loops. Too bad Lismore didn't have a band like that, a band that offered me an immediate future by playing in daylight. The band it did have was for adults and the night.

The Marino was a fox-trot, slow-waltz, quick-step kind of band, strict tempo in the Victor Sylvester manner. The sound was Sylvesterish, as well: Frank Sweeney on mellow tenor-sax, Gandhi Colbert, the ultra-thin station-master, on violin. I don't know who thought up the band's name. I assume, though, that it wasn't the Dublin working-class suburb that was being conjured up but something vaguely Rivierean – balmy evenings, Latin lovers, verandas. . . . They played all the latest, hits by Johnny Ray, Guy Mitchell, Frankie Laine. Their 'Jezebel' was a study in inanition compared to the iron-larynxed tempest of the original, but their 'Roaming round the world / Looking for the sunshine / That never seems to come my way' was definitely *con moto*, and 'The Blue Tango' made a hothouse of many a labourer's brain. They played hops and hurling-club benefits in Cappoquin, Ballyduff, Mocollop, Kilworth, Araglen, and at least once broke the twenty-mile barrier for a date at Watergrasshill.

Chrissy was the pianist, which meant that not only could I take pride in her appearing in public but also that the band sometimes came to Swiss Cottage for rehearsal. And when that happened – usually on the Friday evening before a Sunday date – I was allowed to stay up late. I watched, agog, the instruments being uncased – the golden burnish of the sax rising from its snug, plush groove; the umber varnish of the slender fiddle. And of course, above all, the sacramental assembly of drums and cymbals, the cold gleam of their fixtures, the nipple-headed sticks and chrome brushes, the rap and thud of preparation. How Frankie Walsh tolerated me under his feet, pleading incessantly, 'Can I've a go?' I can't imagine. But he was tolerant to a fault. He'd smile at my desperation, swing me onto his circular, official seat, and try to teach me the crossways grip, all wrist and fingers, that he said was the proper way to play. I was too excited to learn. As far as I was concerned, there was no proper way, there was just playing. My foot couldn't reach the bass-drum pedal, nor my arms all the cymbals, but I didn't care. I bounced up and down on the seat, beat without rhyme or reason those soiled, worn skins that were the colour of a shabby sheep, and felt my whole person turn into a beam.

Once or twice, I remember, I was allowed up extra late – to as unnatural an hour as nine-thirty, perhaps – to sit in on a few numbers. Needless to say, the heater was barred. Obviously I couldn't play it because it was too noisy, but, more important, the heater was a secret between Chrissy and me, and it felt great to have something to keep from Mam. But I was happy to whack a box until Mam poked her head around the parlour door with her, 'Now, Seoirse.'

'Did you hear me?' I demanded, turning to go up the stairs.

'I did, boy,' said Mam: was that a smile in her voice? 'Off with you now.'

And up I scampered, because bed offered more pleasure. I sensed the poor boys of the lane tapping their feet and rhythmically shrugging their shoulders under the street light on the corner opposite. I heard their coarse encomia. I lay safe and warm, humming, and felt delightfully superior to them. And I wanted to shout down to them did they know that was my aunt down there, carrying the melody with airy assurance, plunging into the deep, dark notes with laughing abandon – did they realize that these thoughtless, ticklesome, instantaneous pieces were the real her, my Chrissy? And didn't they glory in it?

I never did shout down, of course. I much preferred to think I had it all to myself, digging my heel into the mattress without ever missing a beat, crooning tune after tune with never, never a stammer over lyrics, waking up after ten the next morning to find the resonance of those ' rittle, sparkling keys inside me, jitterbugging in my veins like thrilling ichor.

Music could be treacherous too, though. I'd already found that out, thanks to the wireless. There was a programme on Athlone (as we called Radio Éireann) every Wednesday lunchtime, 'Hospital Requests'. It was ushered in by a syrupy treatment of Gershwin's 'Someone to Watch Over Me', and, unlike lunchtime listening on other days, had no sponsors and was not introduced by a 'personality' such as Joe Linnane or

15

Dennis Brennan, but by a staff announcer. The show consisted of messages from the well to the ill, accompanied by a piece of music. It was a morbid accessory to our meal, no doubt, but we all enjoyed it, especially when a hospital known to us was mentioned, such as Ardkeen in Waterford City or the Bon Secours in Cork, though Chrissy and Mam often objected that Dublin bias was shown and that if you weren't in Peamount Sanatorium you hadn't a chance of being mentioned. Chrissy and Mam also liked guessing from the name of a far-off hospital, unknown to them, what the patient might be in for. TB always seemed a safe bet.

Sometimes a child would be mentioned, and the women would look lovingly across the table at me and tell me how lucky I was.

'Poor little devil,' they'd say to the radio. 'Think of that, Seoirse; how'd you like to have your birthday in hospital?'

I did think of it. It was horrible. It made me feel very pleased with myself. And – since that was what they seemed to need of me – I felt grateful to my guardians as well: who knows, I thought, only for them I might be stretched out in Ward Z, Pavilion B, this very minute. Then, slap bang in the middle of my complacency, some upsetting song would break through, and I'd burst into tears.

Various singers got to me, and various idioms. Burl Ives doing 'Jimmy Crack Corn', especially the line, 'The master's gone away'. Anything by Kathleen Ferrier struck me as the acme of melancholy (and, as I was often told, she died young). And – the moisturiser *non pareil* – Paul Robeson. He gave me a hell of a time, particularly with 'My Old Kentucky Home'.

That unforgettable song had all the ingredients of definitive water music. 'My Old Kentucky home far away', 'I'm coming', 'Weep no more, my lady', these, combined with the profound lugubriousness of the incomparable Paul, had me howling in no time, howling so inconsolably that there was nothing for it but to turn the thing off until I came to my senses and saw what Chrissy kept telling me was maybe right after all: 'Sure, Seoirse, you're not poor old Joe or anything like it . . .'

If 'My Old Kentucky Home' had been the height of musical treachery, things wouldn't have been so bad. But music had depths of perfidy beyond the range of even Paul Robeson and Stephen Foster, and possessed a power to upset whose sources were much closer to home. In a word, Chrissy was to teach me the piano.

At first I was very excited, imagining that by imitating Chrissy's accomplishments I'd be more like her – carefree, capable, playful, musical: the perfect combination of child and adult, the combination which I longed to perfect. It was good too that Mam considered piano-playing a natural inclination for me, since her encouragement came in terms I could easily identify with. She kept saying how glad I'd be afterwards, and sure a pianist would be welcome anywhere: wouldn't it be grand when, later on, I was 'in company somewhere' (Dublin, of course, that best of all possible worlds) and someone asked if anyone could play. Through the French windows I'd stride, doctors and teachers stepping back to give me access, and out of my head I'd play till dawn – the Cary Grant of Ballsbridge! Simple stardom, that's all I wanted.

I knew the piano was a treasured instrument, and not just because of Chrissy's exploits with the Marino. Not everybody had one, by any means, and ours was kept in the parlour, along with all the other things we didn't really live with: the picture of my father as a baby, the cups, flasks, plates and butter-cooler that Georgie had won running and cycling, the bizarre round table of solid teak, each of whose three curved legs was marked like elephant trunks and faces, minus ears but complete with protruding ivory tusks. And finally, as though in definition of the piano's classiness, we had John Scott-Allen, the organist at the Protestant church, to come and tune ours, the sense of quality deriving from the extreme unusualness of engaging and paying a Protestant to perform a service. Well worth it, though, all agreed, especially when John rewarded us with a five-minute concert when the tuning was done. 'Oh, the light touch of him,' Mam'd exclaim, rapturously. 'By gor, he's another Charlie Kunz.'

So – I had everything going for me. Except myself. I simply couldn't do it. Left hand ingloriously sparred with right, and refused to be reconciled. Melody charmed, bass distracted. Adult coaxed, child sulked. Adult lost patience, child lost temper. Chrissy didn't love me, I *hated* her. I became, on certain grey afternoons, quite simply and unabashedly hysterical. Having to practise, making mistakes, going back over, concentrating. . . . It was all too much for me, too tense,

17

too definitive, too humiliating. I never had to put up with this kind of exposure in school, why should I be subjected to it in pursuit of what was supposed to be a grace and a pleasure? Why had discipline so much to do with it, the lessons so rigorously devoted to limiting options? All the piano had given me before was spontaneity, effervescence, joy: what made the piecemeal approach the one true way?

I had perhaps as many as a dozen lessons in all before my terror and loathing of feeling so vulnerable, so inchoate, so unco-ordinated, won through. Maybe if we'd started with numbers I knew instead of the child's first fingering book – 'bought specially', as I was frequently reminded – and containing tunes which I'd never heard played and which I considered vaguely English and prissy and dull – what was I to 'Baa-baa Black Sheep', or it to me? We should have started, maybe, with the great song my father taught me, 'The Big Rock Candy Mountain'. (But my father was in Dublin.) Or perhaps if we'd been in a less precious room, a place that was less of a shrine and more of a kitchen. . . . Or maybe we should have been a family of Eskimos. . . .

Of all my many tearful tempests, those brought on by the piano lessons bore out best Mam's most frequent criticism of me – 'He can't bear correction.' All the charmless inadequacy of my vanity, impatience and excitability was revealed. The lessons confirmed that I was the cripple that my mother's death and father's absence had made me. I wasn't special, I was hampered. If I was special I'd have been able to sit down and play like Chrissy. Like Chrissy. I didn't want to be myself (the self I might have been had been deferred, uncalled for, by my parents' misfortune); I wanted to be the person who amused me. And now that the main amusement – the airy grace and effortlessness of my beloved's fingers – had grotesquely given way to an implacable logic requiring total selfless surrender, all I could do was sit slumped on the revolving stool in the airless, camphor-tainted parlour and feel music's treason, my face a river of distress, my mind a frenzy of jangling, echoing chords.

So, the lessons were noisily dropped, and not too long afterwards, so were the expressions of disappointment. Chrissy and I were able to be real playmates again. This meant that the drumming and writing resumed, and also that after school we could, every so often, go for walks together.

It was Chrissy who called them walks, and they really were for her benefit, even though we seldom got very far and she had to justify them by saying to Mam, 'It'll give the child an appetite for his tea.' What happened was that Chrissy would saunter down the town, meet someone, or more usually go into some shop (business was always slack on weekday afternoons) and stand there gossiping. Sometimes we'd go farther afield, down the bridge and into the country a little way. Invariably, Chrissy would bump into a boy on these excursions and stand chatting and laughing with him, an unmerciful bore to me, needless to say, much worse than hanging around in Bríd Linneen's or Teasie Meade's where at least I had the chance of getting a sweet to keep me quiet, the sweet accompanied by the warning, 'But don't tell Mam!'

Naturally, it was nice for her to talk to boys, and even I could sense there was an air of getting away with something about those meetings – the speaking in low voices, the half-shocked sound of the giggles. Yet Chrissy seemed more at ease sharing a cigarette and discussing the latest with one of her cronies. And even though she loved a good gossip, I think what she needed from those little outings was not just news. I think she was simply drawn to people who earned their living. She was happy to be in their ambit because it was public, something might happen. Those who stood behind the counter had continuous, varied, socially necessary contact with the world. They weren't exactly subject to the peculiar form of frustration known as being 'at home', twenty-six years old and a mother's help still – the lot of many an unmarried, ill-schooled contemporary of Chrissy's. I would be very sad to think that Chris might ever have felt bitter, or superfluous, or disabled because she couldn't cut soap or draw a cork or, like her friend Alice Luby, be surrounded in the Co-op manager's office with dockets, invoices and Bible-sized ledgers. But it must have been hard for her, day after day, relying for sustenance on domesticity alone (chapel only supervening), deprived of the rewards and distractions of daily life in its social forms, having to ask for the price of a smoke, for money for clothes, having to ask – for all I know – if she could go out with Joe Wall tonight.

Joe Wall. Black hair, dark eyes. Swarthy. Slender. He was   19 from 'down the county', meaning some townland east of Cappoquin, some place we in Lismore didn't have to take seriously: Ballinamult, Modeligo, Affane, some place with just a crossroads, a church and a pub, untouched by rail and only recently electrified. And Joe spoke with the French r's and tormented vowels of his people. We delighted in imitating that accent, Chrissy especially. (She was a mimic of genius. My father, not given to hearty laughter, had tears roll down his cheeks from Chrissy taking off the locals.) 'Deyhre a fayhre in Dun-geayhrvan', we'd say, and convulse with giggles. We felt wonderfully superior: Lismore was *the* place to live. 'Dungarvan is the pisspot of Ireland and Abbeyside the handle', we'd say; and, 'Tallow: the last place God made, and forgot to finish'; and when a thing was crooked it was 'all to one side, like the town of Fermoy'. Better Lismore than any of those places was a widely shared sentiment. But within Lismore, who was at peace, who felt unyearningly at home? Nobody I knew.

Although Joe Wall had the accent of his locality, unlike most people from that part of the world, he didn't screech. His speech was more of a purr. I liked that. It seemed to go with his dark features, and enlarged my sense of his foreignness. And he worked behind the hardware counter in the Co-op. I loved that.

The Co-op was one of my favourite places in the whole town. Georgie bought his Uno paints there, and every Saturday morning I was told to run down to the Co-op for a pound of Clover Meats' best back rashers. As well as the grocery and hardware there was a bar and a yard full of farmers' feedstuffs, and in the yard a cool, tiled room storing eggs and salty homemade butter, a purchase of which Paddy Flynn would slap into shape with the two butter-paddles – silvery motes of salt jumped in the air with every slap. And in the passage leading to the yard there was the barrel.

The barrel frightened and fascinated me. It contained half-heads, pigs' heads split in two. Toothy, prognathous, leering, grey, they floated in thick, unclean-looking brine. The idea of people eating such things alarmed me. No doubt I'm diminished, am somehow less of the people, for never having acquainted my digestion with those salty gargoyles. At Swiss Cottage, the roast beef of old England was our typical Sunday dinner, not jelly and gristle, and proud Mam was to put it on the table, though every so often Geo expressed tiredness of it and called for swine-parts. The fact that people did eat it, though, was fascinating. Many Saturdays I watched in wonder as unknown, untowny women in black shawls descended on the barrel from outlying townlands and hauled out a series of samples, scrutinizing each selection with canny eyes, discerning who knows what succulent potential in the line of a jaw or the flap of a cloven snout. When they were satisfied, they carried their choice, dripping, by the ear into the grocery counter where it was wrapped in a couple of sheets of *The Cork Examiner* and stowed under the purchaser's shawl in a deep, dirty bag.

The hardware was much more sophisticated, to my mind, and I felt more at home there because I associated its turps-tainted air with Georgie. But, as things turned out, I would have been better off trying to talk to those strange pig-fanciers, or getting in the way of the men in the yard and their maledictions. Because what I had to put up with from Joe and Chris was more than I could bear, made me feel as furious and undone as any piano lesson had.

There I'd be, poring over an Uno chart, absorbed by the alleged tonal differences between vermilion and siren-red (I couldn't rightly see; like every other commercial interior of my acquaintance, the hardware was dark). Or I'd be fiddling with hinges or locks or a box of screws, empty-mindedly pleasured by their oily newness. And there'd be this cough. I'd look up. There Chrissy and Joe would be, arms around each other, humming, swaying elaborately in a dance.

Saboteurs! He the dark one, the foreigner, the snake in the grass, impersonator of the Marino's tawdry associations. And she, unspeakably worse, slipping silently into a self beyond me altogether, there in the consummate ordinariness of a slow weekday afternoon.

How dare they! Why did I have to see? And why do it repeatedly? What were they trying to prove?

Time after time I flew at them, puny fists flailing indiscriminately. But I might as well have burst into tears, for all the good my attacks did. 'O!' went Chris and Joe, 'Ow!' – and off they sidled out of range into the dark corner by the never-opened street-door, clutching each other, laughing. And when the

21

laughter stopped I'd hear the scratching of the feet on the shop's coarse floor, and the subtler scratching of cloth on cloth, and the humming – damn music, insufferable signature of all that I was not.

3

'Tottenham Hotspur nil, Aston Vílla nil. Sheffield Wednesday two, Wolverhampton Wanderers one.'

It's Saturday afternoon, and 'Sports Report' is coming in loud and clear on the BBC Light Programme. After the results all the familiar voices will be on hand, gravelly Geoffrey Green, hectic Harold Abrahams, J. Barrington Dalby of the *Daily Mail* on boxing, and of course our host Eamonn Andrews of whom we're all so proud, none more so than Mam (though she hates 'foreign games'): 'Imagine an Irish boy getting on so well in England,' she remarks, hearing his soft Dublin burr, as if he's not doing a job but performing a miracle; as if England for the first generation emigrant is bound to be a loss of public face.

The announcer's litany goes on. 'Scottish League Division Two. Cowdenbeath two, Hamilton Academicals one. Forfar four, Stenhousemuir nil.' The voice is supercilious, unexcitable, giving the impression that its owner didn't give a tinker's curse what happened, and if everyone else did (as they must, otherwise why broadcast?), the more fools they. But in one way it was an ideal voice: it suited the vaguely ecclesiastical design of the wireless, a Philco, its rounded top, circular dial and curved strips of wood across the cloth of the speaker making it look like a little tabernacle. What more appropriate voice could come out of it than one sounding at least as well trained as a Redemptorist's?

The Philco suffered horribly from static, though, for which incontinence – as involuntary, unmalicious and unpredictable as bedwetting – it received traditional treatment: beating. 'East Fife five--kraak!' Mouthing a selection of oaths Georgie sprang up from the newspaper, into which he'd been studiously copying the scores, and with the broad of his palm, lambasted the hapless instrument.

'Thunder in the air,' I said (my father told me that).

'Thunder my arse,' said Geo in a low growl, not looking at me, readjusting his spectacles and returning to the paper. How could I contradict him? He was as much father to me as Chrissy was mother.

Besides, I knew better than to talk to him during 'Sports Report'. Being stymied by static was one thing, but the distraction of a know-nothing child was much more than he should be asked to bear. Interrupting an abstruse discussion about Walter Winterbottom's next Eleven or the fate of the All Blacks with some uncontainable irrelevance about my day's doings, elicited a roar which froze me.

Silence was a mortifying condition for me at the best of times, as I firmly believed that whatever crossed my mind had to be aired immediately, if not sooner. Moreover, I belonged to a household where there was continual clamour for free speech, and for free speech in its definitive form at that, namely, the last word. So, why shouldn't I be able to put in my spoke when I wanted? I had such good questions, too. How would you get a job on the wireless? Why had the teams such funny names (Accrington Stanley, Crewe Alexandra)? And above all – one to which I still don't have a good answer – why did Geo take down all the results?

There were two sorts of results, soccer and racing. The soccer ones were easy to record, because the fixtures were set out in the papers with spaces for the numbers to be entered. I was even allowed to do it sometimes. Georgie would ferret out the butt of a pencil from his overalls and bark at me to carry on. But the racing results – more exotic names: Uttoxeter, Haydock Park, Doncaster, Goodwood – were much more difficult, and were one of the reasons Geo so fiercely insisted that I sing dumb.

The runners and riders were set out in the paper according to no pattern that I could discern. Hedged around by form numbers, weights, trainers' and owners' names, Georgie had to look sharp to mark those who figured at the finish. His pencil would chase up and down the list, trying to keep pace with the announcer, a game of concentrated co-ordination in itself, its impatient and slightly obsessive character high-lighted and preserved by being conducted in silence.

It has occurred to me since that George noted the vagaries of horseflesh to inform and console the chronic punters whom he'd certainly run into later on, drinking at Madden's. Maybe they gambled on the Football Pools too, though I think the Pools were outlawed in Ireland. Still, with so much coming and going between England and Lismore I suppose enrolment in one would be easy to arrange. But if the Pools were illegal why did the national dailies provide space to record the scores? I have no answer. It's one of those things that belongs truly in the past, beyond interpretation and intractably its useless, undiminished self.

The results were not the only, or even the main, reason for the rule of silence, however. The main reason was that Georgie loved to argue. I've never met a man to relish disagreeing like him. It wasn't so much that he believed everyone else to be wrong and he alone right, though that was part of his irrepres-sible yen to wrangle. In addition, his arguing desired to demonstrate that he was more authoritative than anyone else. If an illustrious cross-channel pundit mentioned the genius of Marciano, Georgie would snap back with, 'What about Tony Zale? He'd Louis on the ropes in the twelfth. Only for a lucky punch . . .' He'd flare up in defence of Dr Pat Callaghan whenever the latest feat in the field was discussed. Gordon Richards had his good points no doubt, but no jockey could compare to Charlie Smirke.

In all the cries of 'Bunkum!' and 'Arra, what ails you!' that punctuated those radio hours there was a very complex reaction. First of all, obviously, Georgie was an insatiable sports fan. If it ran, walked, drove, swam or cycled, it was Georgie's friend. As well as that, and perhaps this is where the results'-noting comes in, he absolutely loved to be up to the minute, ahead of tomorrow's papers, in the know. I think, too, that he often despised the dispassionate clubland tones of some radio 'personalities', annoyed at the thought of their soft money and cushy jobs, and by the fact that though they'd seen so much, their outlook and perspective wasn't worth a curse. Those plausible, ineffectual voices lacked all that Georgie's possessed – ardour, passion, faith – but with which it could accomplish so little. Over and above the need to top every received opinion and reported occasion with one of his own, there seemed to be a more powerful, less articulate desire for voice itself. His arguing was an assertion of the legitimacy of arguing, of telling it straight, of extolling the legend and affronting the hack, of disagreeing without the air heaving with tension and rancour as it did in the kitchen when he and Mam went at it.

Compared to how petrified I felt during those personal set-to's, sharing 'Sports Report' in silence wasn't too bad at all. Georgie and I were on our own, in the dining-room (that's where the radio was kept, along with the good china, my parents' wedding-picture, the photo of me in my First Communion suit by Stritch of Fermoy, and the oleograph of a slant-eyed Lady of Perpetual Succour). Geo covered the table with the daily papers, a gesture both business-like and anarchic – and impossible in the kitchen. He pushed his battered soft hat, speckled with paint and plaster, back off his forehead, and his pipe smouldered sweetly. The women were in the kitchen getting tea ready, but we were men together, attending to men's business, which of course sport exclusively was, as much so as, if not more than, going out to work. And naturally once I knew silence was obligatory I made sure not to break it, not wanting to be shouted at, obviously, but also indulging in the narcissistic satisfaction of deliberately being good.

It seems now that the easiest thing would have been for Georgie simply to forbid me the room because of his craving to hear. 'Run away out and play;' everybody said it. But he didn't, not at five on Saturday afternoons, anyhow. Maybe he too thought of us as men together. Or did he imagine that exposure to world sports headlines would fill me with the desire to feature among them one day? Alas, I became a fan, not an athlete, and a hollow fan what's more, my mind full of trivia. Unlike George, I haven't been able to create a world-view from statistics and affections. I'm too watchful of myself to be so idiosyncratic, so outspoken.

As to maleness, well, Georgie was erratically interested in making a man of me. He made me climb to the crest of the roof of the Presbyterian church once (by ladder: he was working up there). All I could see as I clung to the ridge-tiles were trees. I felt cheated. A better idea of his was to call me 'Mike'. I was very pleased by this. The name I was known by in those days was 'Seoirse' ('Shore-sha'), which I disliked enormously. Nobody in Lismore could pronounce it: 'Shosho' was the best they could do. And the gratings over the holes into which rain from the gutters drained were called shores. And I was called it for what I considered to be the wrong reasons – as the first male grandchild, I had to be named for my father's father; and with two Georges already in the house ahead of me I had to be different to prevent confusion. Tradition and convenience did not provide the basis I needed for identifying with what I was called.

So, I found it ticklesome to speculate about what being a Mike would be. Stocky. Hard as nails. Filthy. Poorly dressed. Reared on the street. A child of the people. His house was a warm cabin in Botany or Church Lane. And of course he was great at games. I liked him a lot. But the more I thought about him the more I realized how well Seoirse suited me – obscure, uncommon, unfamiliar. That, I felt sure, was me *really*. I couldn't be a Mike, even for Georgie. I don't know if he ever accepted this: he did, I feel, in a desperate, inarticulate way want me to be his little boy – a way which I now crystallized in our silent camaraderie, a condition of legitimacy then, of true fracture now.

To breathe Georgie's smoke, to practise perfect obedience, to be – however vaguely and uncomprehendingly – abreast of the latest, gave me a delightful sense of attachment. But by far the best thing was that it was only a preamble to the evening ahead, when the same sense would, thanks to Geo, come fully into its own for an hour or two.

From 'Sports Report' onwards, everything went according to a different pattern from that of other days. Tea wasn't the same because Geo wasn't late in from work and needing his main meal. And instead of the usual bread, butter and homemade jam of workaday evenings, on Saturdays we had a selection of buns by Thompson's of Cork, delivered fresh to Noey Greehy's just a few hours before. Buns with cream in the middle, jam doughnuts that leaked deliciously when least expected, and a strange suety raisiny species of gingerbread called Chester-cake. We'd have one each, and maybe Geo would be offered a boiled egg and a slab of Golden Vale processed cheddar as well.

'Quite a party!' our expressions exclaimed, smirking through the sugar and smears. And indeed those teas were about as relaxed as we ever managed to be together. It was the buns that did it. We were all perfectly conscious of what a concession to irresponsibility they represented. To pay good money for what you should be able to make yourself at quarter the cost was an immense affront to Mam's idea of domestic economy. We never went in for cakes by Gateaux or such frivolity. Make what you need was Mam's philosophy. She mistrusted the readymade – the machine-knit sweater and the tinned vegetable were anathema to her. How could anyone be a decent housewife and avail of such costly and labour-saving items? I asked her once why we couldn't have some of the relishes that seemed to flow freely through the meals my playmates had. She was horrified. 'Them old things are only to cover up bad cooking,' she told me. And, later, having thought more about it: 'It's only drunkards like them, the spicy taste makes 'em mad for another drink, and that's all they want.' This I couldn't dispute. I'd noticed that whenever Geo brought home a jar of mixed pickles there were blunders and mumbles late on the stairs for several nights afterwards. Of course, the telling-off he received for buying something 'out of his own pocket' instead of from Mam's well-watched kitty – for, in effect, pleasing himself – might well have contributed to the making of his step-missing gait.

That kitty, which came from Georgie's weekly earnings, often caused Saturday evening squalls. Mam used to get it into her head every once in a while to challenge the size of it. Georgie would be accused of keeping more back for himself than was right. He'd counter-attack that he was being begrudged a drink now, what would it be next, tobacco? These skirmishes always ended by his storming off, slamming doors.

They're more upsetting to think of now than they were to witness then. George could contradict the BBC and all belonging to it, but he never managed to outface his mother. It was as though her widowhood gave her a moral strength, a power over him, that he couldn't withstand. Her manlessness was a constant, unspoken taunt, reminding him that, in her eyes, he would never be the man his father was. Never the tradesman, never the provider, never the authority. Her George had only one equal: herself. And not all the shouting and slamming in the world could infuse Geo with an antidote to her view and reassure him that he was real enough as he stood.

What annoyed me at the time about these wrangles is that they occurred at the worst possible moment, just as Saturday evening was about to reach the climax of its specialness. Everything so far had been building nicely. After tea, Georgie shaved. A kettle was boiled specially, the kitchen sink was placed entirely at his disposal, down with the wooden razor-case and its delicate petal-shaped snap, out with the razor from its velvet nest. An intricate twirl, sheer steel gleaming in evening light, and a new blade was inserted. Then the shaving mug, the face santa-claused with lather, the head immobilized in a succession of odd poses, and snick, snick, snick . . .

A radio-knob, a mass-produced bun, the glint of a razor: the workaday surrendered itself to, begat, an alternative, restorative pace and idiom. That's what made Saturday so special, those hours of recuperation, as though peace was being made with the week's toil. Much better than Sunday, when rest was official: secular adequacy insinuated itself more naturally than compulsory worship. Mam's challenge to shiny-cheeked, clean-shirted Georgie was a refusal to believe in the minuscule, delightful heresy of a kitchen miracle. And just when he and I were about to set off on our delicious pilgrimage to the library, too!

Georgie was a terror to read. During Lent once, in a spirit of exquisite satire, he gave up everything – smoking, drinking, going to the cinema, sugar in his tea – and sat in evening after evening reading. The women resented it, being unused to not having the house to themselves, but Geo read on remorselessly, a book a night for forty nights.

This was not usual, though, sitting in our midst reading, placing himself in a kind of purdah which we had to admit but felt to be untrue. There was no need to be so pointedly 'good'; it wasn't being good at all, it was only a response to Mam's criticisms of what a derelict Christian he was. A pity he didn't have as well thought out a reponse to her other criticisms.

Typically, Georgie was a closet reader. He read in bed. No matter how late it was, he told me once, when he got home he couldn't sleep without reading. He read by flashlight, or rather by bicycle lamp. Exhausted batteries accumulated on the dressing-table until Chrissy, the bedmaker, threw them all out, fresh ones included, causing great ructions, Georgie being extremely sensitive to the idea of being tampered with. (He really raised the roof if one of his newspapers was mislaid and unavailable when he came in from work.)

I don't know why he didn't use the electric light. My sense of Mam suggests that she complained to him once about running up the light bill. Her strength, her reality, consisted in being prepared not to bend about issues of this kind, causing the objects of her criticism to invent very elaborate rationales and self-justifications in order to assimilate what was pure, unmitigated, small-mindedness.) His response, along the lines of his Lenten demonstration, was to deny her for ever after the basis for such an accusation, making her inflexibility his own, attaining (like a true Irishman) freedom through deprivation.

On the other hand, my sense of Georgie suggests that he used the lamp so's not to have to get out of bed to switch off the ceiling light. Getting up again was a nuisance to be sure; but better to have poor light and awkward position than undergo a fifteen-second dash across freezing lino to the switch and back? Yes: Because this was the way he decided to do it, the way (for all I know) he may have hit on as a youngster, when lights out meant something. A way nobody else would dream of, so how dare anyone criticize it?

And what didn't Geo read? Well, first of all, newspapers. Three dailies, *Press*, *Independent*, *Cork Examiner*. Two weeklies, *Dungarvan Observer* and *Waterford Star*. Eight Sundays! Two Irish, *Press* and *Independent*. Six English: *Graphic*, *Empire News*, *People*, *Sunday Express*, *Dispatch* and *Chronicle*. These he devoured after first mass and breakfast, as though starving for them. He loved to read out juicy morsels to us, savouring the gossip of the stars, grunting 'Good God' at the 'human goat' type of bizzarerie which, according to Fleet Street, constituted life in the English provinces.

What else did he read? *Wide World*, which had pictures of crocodile-eating Eurasians, or vice-versa, on the cover. *Ring Magazine* – bearish Archie Moore, squat Hogan Bassey, Carmen Basilio's eye, like a blue-red orange, after lithe Sugar Ray had finished with it. Don Cockle, thrashed in California. He read Nat Gould, Edgar Wallace, Leslie Charteris, Peter

29

Cheyney. Westerns by the dozen. War books: *Two Eggs on My Plate*, *The White Rabbit*, *They Have Their Exits* by Airey Neave. Geo's taste a lust for action in a world of talk. With my hand in his thick calloused hand – down by the dim lights of Main Street's stores, past the gaggle of old men and boys gossiping around the Monument, up Gallow's Hill – I felt my face aglow with the thought of being in this strong man's keeping, safe and sound in the feeling that he, at least, belonged in the world beyond the home.

The library was on Gallow's Hill (locals said 'Gallus'). It looked like it was on the edge of town because, apart from the National Bank opposite, there was nothing near it. In front, the road sloped off to Tallow, westwards. Behind, some of the Castle Farm ran away to the river, protected by a tall stone wall: private – keep out. Botany was close by, of course, and came out onto the main road farther west, but it was largely obscured by the bank and bank garden, and besides, it and the library had little in common.

Officially New Street, Botany was a straggle of cabins built when transportation to Australia was the judicial rage. Apparently moving – or being moved – into them struck a contemporary wit as joke exile. Now the street was anything but new, its homes wan and world-weary where they weren't dilapidated. They didn't look quite as bad as the ones in the poverty zone at our end of town, Church Lane, but it was only a matter of time till they did.

From such façades – and indeed from the peeling, washed-out fronts of Main Street – the library seemed a world away. It was neat and trim: red brick and white painting. It sat above street level, on top of steps, behind a gate and railings. It had parquet floors and leaded windows. It enjoined quiet. I had no trouble thinking of it ecclesiastically, though its size made it closer kin to that other mainstay of national architectural ambition, the bungalow.

I was very impressed, in addition, by the fact that the library had a special status independent of the one I conferred on it. (As usual, if something pleased me it had to be special. Pleasure, the satisfaction of desire, the matching of world to need: these were not to be thought of as commonplace.) The library was the headquarters of the County Library service, and to prove it had a large, green, lumbering Bedford van which Andy Drohan drove out to the branches, reminding them of Lismore's superiority.

The idea of siting the County Librarian's office in Lismore has, for me now, a peculiar period feel. I can see some ardent civil servant in the early days of the Free State deciding on it. And it was an imaginative decision, though I find it sad as well as endearing. Lismore is one of those special Irish places to have its own book (like Kells or Durrow). Therefore, shouldn't such a place, sanctified by learning and culture in the days when your average Brit was still attempting to master the bow and arrow (or so we were encouraged to believe), be the town of the Book once more?

Indeed, what could be more appropriate? It's debatable, however, if the people of the town were able to see themselves and their birthplace as others saw them. They all were aware of Lismore's ancient history, knew of the Book, the Crozier, the fact that the immediate spiritual satrap was Bishop of Waterford *and Lismore*. But you can't eat ancient history. Let the civil servant be as imaginative as bedamned. Let his gesture be a perfect embodiment of the prevailing cultural orthodoxy. What did it profit the man on the corner? Sweet damn-all. He and his countless brothers would have much preferred a future instead of a past; if possible one that didn't start with the boat to England. Sadly what Dublin sent down was a gesture, a posture, a notion – not a daily wage out of which the man on the corner could evolve his own cultural vocabulary.

To make matters worse, there was nothing in the library that might make me relish what lay behind officialdom's nod in our direction. There weren't any children's books in stock that I remember about the legendary heroes, their derring-do and sexiness. All I was interested in was the action-packed latest, doing my best to mimic Georgie's tastes. If a book didn't contain an aeroplane or a launch, I wouldn't go near it. I did choke down some of the classics – *Kidnapped, Martin Rattler* – and grudgingly acknowledged their story-interest. But as a general principle I rejected reading chosen for me by adults. That principle, as well as my craving for contemporaneity, must account for my lack of interest in the heroic-past-in-pictures books that my father brought down to me for Christmas once or twice. At any rate, their larger-than-life figures 31 never really appealed to me then. The life-sized took my fancy. If I had to have heroes, let them be legitimate heroes, like Biggles, or the Yank who floated down the Amazon on balsa wood in *The Seven Little Sisters*, a great book made even better by the fact that I got it from the library to keep, a tattered treasure, withdrawn from circulation, which Georgie brought home for me one time he was renovating one of the inner rooms. As long as the library provided a steady flow of latter-day heroics, I was content, and when Georgie said approvingly, 'Looks like a good one' (*Tiger Mountain* by Angus MacVicar), my Saturday was complete.

I found it hard to accept that Georgie's wasn't. Whereas I could now float home and sink myself pleasurably into some hotbed of foreign intrigue (the best thing about evil was that it always took place in a good climate – subliminal acknowledgement of the devil's omnipotence: he brought his normal working conditions with him on his terrestrial visits), Georgie's Saturday evening was just beginning. I suppose I didn't feel entirely comfortable with the thought that he was grown up, and wanted to be out and about doing grown-up things. All the more so since going drinking, which is what he did, was the cause of so much ill-feeling, Mam objecting bitterly to his keeping the company of the spongers, bums and leeches who, in her dreadful vision of Lismore's night-life, infested the bars of the town.

In one literal sense, Mam's objection was all too accurate. Apart from the shopkeepers, who didn't drink or if they did lost their shops, and the professional people, who kept their drinking to themselves, pickling their livers while they preserved their status, there weren't all that many with enough in their pockets to drink whenever they wanted. Some, perhaps, didn't have the stomach to defy their mothers week in, week out. But for the most part, there weren't that many common citizens with regular work. A few postmen, a handful working at the Castle, a very small number of tradesmen: these were the regular earners. As for the rest, grave-digging, clearing up after a storm, helping out at threshing and beet-snagging, a day here, a day there, filling in their time with Public Assistance and begetting children on wives shaped like steamrollered mattresses . . .

Georgie bewailed the lack of work, too. Only for the

goodwill his father had created among the gentry, he might well have found the going harder. Not that it was easy. The gentry were dying out. And Georgie could be heard complaining loud and long that shopkeepers couldn't be relied on for sixpence. He redecorated their nameboards, repointed their chimneys, resashed the windows of their heavily furnished, under-used upstairs apartments. But getting them to pay was like getting blood from a turnip. And as for farmers: they were as bad, if not worse. What they couldn't botch together themselves had to be paid for in bags of potatoes or maybe a goose at Christmas. At least the gentry, whatever else about them, paid cash on the nail.

So Mam was right. There were a lot of men in the town in need of a drink, and in need of the price of one. But she was wrong too. The very companions that she named as the biggest spongers were the ones Georgie needed most, the old stagers of the town, waiting out their time in some married daughter's houseful of squally nippers or alone in unkempt, cold-hearthed cottages. If they couldn't sit down for a drink and a chat at this hour of their lives, the world was a dead loss altogether, was Geo's attitude. It pleased him to know he could please these old lads: as he told me afterwards, he felt at home with them. Mam was wrong because she refused to admit this, refused to see that Georgie had needs which only he could satisfy – or if she saw that, didn't want the choice of forms to be at his discretion.

Geo's aim was not just to please, however. He wasn't sly enough to patronize people. He needed not approval, but talk. In the low, smoky, sour-smelling room the old codgers' moist voices reminisced away. Experiences were resurrected and opinions dusted down. They became men again, tearing and dragging for some toff's steward, poaching the Duke's salmon under a sovereign-coloured springtime moon. Nutty Keating, Geo's favourite, a stone-mason with a belly like a sandbag, gave tips about granite and told stories of travelling the country raising churches. His finest hour was the time he spent on the cathedral at Queenstown, as he still called it, looking out over the droves of youngsters like himself setting sail for America, thinking how lucky he was to have a chisel for an anchor.

But everyone in Lismore had been lucky 'in them days', 33

before the Great War, 1916 and all that. There was lashings of work, and porter was only a ha'penny a pint. Miss Curry shipped out flowers from the town that bedecked the breasts of London debutantes. Paxton had his butter factory. The clogmill was going strong. You could hardly cross the street for the bustle and jam of horses and carts.

'Ah Jesus, there was some life in it then.' Even I, doing nothing to seek out old-timers' musings, was familiar to yawning-point with this refrain. What it meant to Georgie to pursue and absorb its most stirring settings and minutest variations I can only guess. But pursue them he did. He would no more dream of neglecting Nutty or Cuggar Whelan or Marsh Reagan or John the Bird than he would the library or me. Perhaps we were all mixed up together in his mind.

Or was it that he was patiently piecing together memory, impression, animus and fact in order to get precisely right the lineaments of the limbo into which the town had declined? Or was the insufficiency of the present softened by the continual review of the amount of life that had gone into making it? No doubt he loved the old lore for its own sake, the romance of other days unrehearsed and vivid on the tongue – who had threatened bloodshed for a half-acre of hillside, whose daughters had never married and why? Was it true that the big-shots down the river used to hold Orange conclaves? Loved it, yes, but did he make anything of it? Or is to love not to make anything more, but to rest in a state of indiscriminate, unadulterated acceptance, each story sufficient to the evening of its telling? All I know is that he flew in Mam's face more flagrantly for the sake of those pensioners that he did for many an ostensibly more personal cause. With a son's ache, he seemed to lust after what he couldn't live.

'G'night, Mike!' he'd cry.

But before I'd raised my head from my new book to shout my own glad, thankful, 'Night, Mike!', the front door was slammed, and he was off into the adult night, headlong and hungering.

II

CORNERS

1

A great thing happened when I was ten: I stopped sleeping in the same room as Chrissy and Mam and got a room of my own. 'The girls' room,' it was called, and it was also the room in which Dad (my grandfather, that is) had had his final illness. But these associations didn't bother me. I was too busy acting independent.

I got the room after my bad dreams died down, maybe as a reward, or maybe as an expression of relief on the part of Mam and Chris. Although I haven't had them since, I remember those dreams very vividly, and I remember they went on for a long time, not every night, but very often, for well over a month. Nightmares about my legs being cut off alternated with a truly terrifying sensation of being upside-down in bed. I can't see now why a sense of having head and heels reversed should be so awful. At the time, however, it gave me feelings of dreadful molestation, as though I was the sport of incomprehensible forces.

I know my crying out and quivering caused disquiet because Mam eventually came up with something to blame for it. According to her, my condition was the result of a seaside holiday I spent with Granny Royce (my mother's mother), my father, and one of my Wexford cousins, Patrick Askins. We spent three weeks together in a bungalow belonging to other cousins, the Morans, at a place called Ballyvaldan, near Blackwater, County Wexford.

'That lonesome ould place,' said Mam, reprovingly, having never been within fifty miles of it.

She had a point, though. I wasn't happy there. I felt I was being cheated out of three weeks of my father's exclusive attention in bustling Dublin. But I never thought it so bad that   37 nightmares should be my principal souvenir. Even if I was afraid of the water (and had my fear shown up by Patrick, who was not only braver but younger), Blackwater was interesting. There was its name, for one thing: the same name as the river in Lismore, yet it didn't have a river in it. Strange. There was a shop there that sold ice-cream, owned by a family named Fortune, and when the daughter of the house served us, my father always said, 'Was that Miss Fortune?' and I laughed and laughed. And there was Dempsey, whose car we hired to take us back to Enniscorthy, where Granny Royce and Patrick lived. He had a habit of saying, 'Be the gob o' man!' whatever you said to him, and he whirled his Consul round the unpaved backroads with a flourish. I loved him.

So, I don't know what got on my nerves. Maybe whatever it was didn't emerge till I got back to Lismore, because I wouldn't have been able to trust anyone except Mam with it. Or perhaps what upset me was returning itself. The holiday household – father, (grand) mother, brotherly cousin – was a closer facsimile of what I wanted. But it turned out, after all, to be only a rehearsal, a game of happy families, and shockingly short-lived.

But I got the room. And very proud I was of it as well. It was mine, mine! Before long, whenever the atmosphere in the kitchen disagreed with me, I threatened to withdraw upstairs, completely, to live alone as much as possible, to become in fact what history and fortune had fashioned me, a man apart.

It wasn't until years later, when I was fourteen or fifteen and home from boarding-school (by which time both Georgie and Chrissie had at last left home and – since I was seeing less of my father – I had Mam all to myself more or less all summer long), that the room really did become a retreat. In the early days of my occupancy, however, the best thing about it was that I now had my own window on the world. On the lean uplands of furzey Shrough sun and cloud composed a child's painting of green, brown and yellow. Farther up, a blue shoulder of Knockmealdowns sloped westward in shy hurry. Every so often I'd spend an hour lost in those far-off colours.

There was such scenery around Lismore, though, that I took it for granted. The pride of mountains and the massiveness of woods was not what overawed me. The street opposite my window sufficed for that, supplying as much as I desired of mystery, sympathy, terror and play. Church Lane. When I think of it now I think not only of a lost playground and all the poor people whose poor homes were there (that's what overawed me, really, their nothingness); I think too that it was the town in essence, Lismore in its bare bones. And with my room facing directly onto it I came to believe that the view contained, or illustrated, something about myself, and that I'd been appointed to the room in order to find out what that was. Something along those lines must have crossed my mind. I spent so many rainy afternoons staring down that mean street. I could look straight down and see everything. Often I felt as melancholy at the sight as if I'd been looking down a ward in a hospital.

The lane was L-shaped, skirting around behind the north side of East Main Street and coming out at the gates of the Protestant church, hence the name – officially Church Street, christened no doubt by the man who owned it, and most of the town besides, the Duke of Devonshire. I could only see the long arm of the L, down as far as Dunne's, the ball-alley, and Doherty's, though as I gazed I had the whole of the lane in mind. The right-hand side, going down, consisted of a row of one-storey cabins (in the lower lane, out of sight, these were fronted by square, squat, slate-roofed porticoes). On the left there were some cabins too, to start with, and then a gap where some two-storey houses had stood when I was small. They had been condemned, though (a term which had put me in mind of disease), and knocked down. All that remained was a hole in the side of the street, a pile of yellowish rubble speck-led with scraps of paint and burgeoning colonies of nettles and dockleaves.

'An eyesore.'

'Well, 'tis true for you, it is an eyesore.'

Adult opinion was unanimous. But nobody did anything about it. We youngsters were glad the rubble remained, because it made great cowboy country, the finest network of gulches and passes around.

Opposite that pile of failed housing stood the tap. There was only one in the lane (and the same was true in Botany and Chapel Street). Early and late, whenever I looked, some woman could be seen staggering off with a brimming bucket in each hand, arms wavering slightly in inarticulate 39 semaphore. Everyone else in the town had piped water. Only poor people had to fetch and carry in order to wash and eat. It was strange. I couldn't imagine how money and water mixed.

It was the same way with electricity. The town transformer was down the street from the tap in Boyle's field, just by the ball-alley. Its clean, silent energy was a wonder to me, and I liked its abstract hum. Raised above us, resplendent in coils and condensers, it struck me that it could well be an idol for a tribe that didn't have one – the English, maybe; I was always hearing at home how godless they were. But marvellous as electricity might be, there was many a household in the lane and elsewhere whose kitchens it never brightened, and where candle and oil-lamp shone on uneclipsed.

No doubt I felt drawn to the lane because of the strange state of its light and water. Such conditions made the place seem another country, hardly Ireland at all, but some dilapidated, unrenewable zone quite out of touch and out of keeping with the place the risen people called their own. I must have wondered idly what kind of people these cabin-dwellers were, really: how they bore being so different from Main Street? It was impossible not to be struck by the unbridgeable, inscrutable gulf which the mere turn of a corner could evidently create. But to be drawn thus was only to be vaguely drawn, the product of solitary upstairs musings, those moods in which I saw more clearly than anything else the strangeness of the world and the arbitrary formulae of its dispositions. Usually I was too busy playing down the lane, with the lads of the lane, to bother my head about differences.

We played in the ball-alley. That was the lane's greatest draw. A rectangular court with a front wall perhaps twenty foot high, and side walls sloping down from it until they levelled off at say seven feet, the alley was undoubtedly one of Lismore's great amenities. It was built before the Great War, when the lane was a far different place (as Mam made sure I knew). I imagine the idea was to anticipate or deflect the work that the devil is said to make for idle hands. But partly, too, the alley represented a piece of cultural assertion typical of its genera-tion. It must have taken a certain amount of guts (a virtually incalculable amount to those in my day whom the low state of the town's morale left feeling high and dry) to erect a Gaelic games facility right in the town on land which presumably had to be bought, land which might well have been earmarked for a couple more rent-yielding cabins. The inspiration to build it was possibly supplied by the Ramblers, Lismore's football team of the day, who (I quote Mam's attitude) were just about world-famous and beat the best of them. Yet to find a field to play on they had to settle for a thistly semi-hill some miles along the Ballyduff road. So, I suppose, now that I think of it, we played our ball in an historical monument.

The Gaelic game we played was handball. We didn't play it properly – I was about to add, automatically, 'of course'; what was there in the town that didn't leave something to be desired? There was no club. Normally, handball affairs would be under the same aegis as those of hurling and football. Nobody doubted that it was a Gaelic game, of course. It wouldn't surprise me to learn that some nationalist ideologue has traced its Indo-European roots, noting along the way handball's similarity to the Basques' *pelote* (and, wasn't it from that part of the world the Tuatha de Danaan came north to fashion us), not to mention Pakistani expertise at squash – those are the lads from the Indus valley, aren't they, the cradle of Celtdom itself. But, for once, national wasn't synonymous with seriousness and organization. Not the least pleasure of the alley was that we were left to carry on as best we could, and had only ourselves to please. In this one case, neglect was enlightened.

There being no club, we had no way of acquiring the proper balls to play with, the standards, as they were called: there was a softball standard, which merely stung the palm off your hand, and a hardball, a small rock about the size of a squash ball which, when struck, jarred every tissue between wrist and fingertip. Not only did nobody have the money to buy these official projectiles, the shopkeepers of the town knew it and never bothered to stock them. Though, even if we had them to play with it wouldn't have done us much good, since they would have been too lively for an alley without a back wall. For, as though designed with a view to articulate incompleteness, that's what our alley lacked. A ball with the life of a standard in it would have ended up among the porticoes every toss. So, since nobody was going to provide us with a wall to confine the bounce, we made do happily with superannuated 41 tennis balls and lumps of sponge as lively as brick.

Once, I remember, an effort was made to put handball on a more public footing. It was always acknowledged that we would never produce anyone like the Ryans and Doyles of Wexford, or Kirby of Clare. But couldn't we, for God's sake, try to make the game less of a hand-to-mouth thing, with maybe a town tournament and neutral markers. And why not usher in the new age with an exhibition match, a proper singles challenge, best-of-five . . . . The planning and anticipation had the anxiety of a prayer about them. I don't know who the two who played the exhibition were, strangers from down the county, probably (there was a beautiful alley in Loughmore, the poor quarter of Dungarvan; it had a *glass* back wall so the people in the adjoining stand – *a stand!* – didn't miss a move). But I remember that they paraded up the main street and down the lane, followed by a large throng, and led, strange to behold, by the massed melodeons of the three Keatings, Pad Tierney, I think, drumming, and beating the shine off a triangle, an old soak from Botany who went by the name of Jim Slog. The melodeons' suspirations had a sarcastic drawl to them, the crowd was beery and rambunctious, and I would like to think that there was a jeer at respectable, do-nothing Main Street in the whole thing.

We all enjoyed the exhibition, but nothing ever came of it. Either we needed a more exalted inspiration, or were too set in our informal ways to bother with leagues and the like, or perhaps there was a question of who would supply the shorts and singlets which were necessary if we were to become official, judging by what the two imported contestants wore. The lads I played with hardly had a shoe to their foot or a seat to their trousers. And when I hear again, now, the slap of running feet in rainy streets, or see the white of private flesh, I realize that it wasn't really the alley that I was drawn to, much as I enjoyed handball (not least the discovery that there was a game I could play), but crossing the line to consort with the impoverished, sharing for a couple of hours their looser, unstylized, more dangerous life.

I envied them. I had the beige, hand-knit sweaters and the cotton socks. But they had strength and fury and staying-power. Nobody told them they had to do homework or to sit quiet and read a book – sensibly, since where would stillness get them? So they had plenty of time to develop their prowess at handball and catapulting and soccer, attraction to which was inspired by all the brothers and neighbours who came home from England. It made good sense to favour soccer. Sooner or later – and usually sooner – every youngster in the lane was bound for the boat. And they never made the grade hurling, largely because so few of them could afford to buy a stick. (A rubber soccer ball was a lot cheaper and lasted a lot longer.)

And could those boys play handball? Day after day, game after game, they flammed ball against wall with untiring ease. They always ran me ragged when I played against them, and when I played with them, in doubles, I hardly got a shot, because their timing and alley-sense enabled them to anticipate whatever might come my way. But I accepted that they were streets ahead of me, admired them for it, thought of them as stars (the brightness of their vigour, their inexhaustibility). Often I went down to the alley just to look on.

A summer afternoon. I've placed myself gingerly – afraid of my life that I'll dirty my trousers – on the bald hillock opposite the alley. The players toss, for serve. At once I'm lost to – immersed in, stupefied by – this paupers' ballet. Blur of arm and ball, disputatious call ('Short!', 'Hinder!'), slap and smack of rubber rifled against stone. Except it's hard to think of poverty. (Afternoon inches by, bodies whirl undimmed.) Are these the lesser orders, the ones, who, I've been told, must live on only bread and tea, whose mothers scurry sheepishly up to the convent with a tin to ask for the charity of leavings, whose fathers will do no work heavier than elbow-exercises at Grock Foley's bar? They were not indeed! They were light, blithe, vivid – *life*!

Nor was this experience of them confined to the ball-alley. It was there when Eddy Cooney showed me how to make a bird-lime (make a paste from the pith of alder, smear it on a twig; when the bird lands there, he sticks, so you can catch him). It was there watching them shoulder home a limb after a storm, or a *brusna* (a bundle of brambles and deadwood typically the size of a miniature haystack). The leavings of the Duke's plantations; sole means of keeping the home fires burning. It was there when I saw Des Callaghan or Tom   43

Lenane trudging down Main Street with their overflowing buckets of whorts and blackberries, grinning at the spoils of the day, at the cash Bob Nolan was going to give them, at the sixpenny ice-cream that was to be their main reward, the rest being required for bread.

And above all it came to me on Stephen's day when the poor boys of the whole parish – and most prominently to me, of course, my lane buddies – took to the streets as wren boys.

Stephen's morning was one of the few times of the year when the whole household in Swiss Cottage stayed in bed late. Mam didn't get up for mass, nobody worked, and the house conveyed a delicious air of somnolence as I settled into one of my Christmas books, partly no doubt because it held more people – Peggy and my father down from Dublin, Frankie or Elizabeth home from England. But then – smash – right in the middle of the heavy-lidded peace – Bang, Bang, Bang! – the wren boys at the door.

They knocked and knocked, blowing their new tin whistles, harmonicas and kazoos, pausing only to deliver their chant:

> The wren, the wren, the king of all birds,
> St Stephen's Day he was caught in the furze.
> Up with the kettle and down with the pan;
> Tuppence or thruppence to bury the wren.
> All silver and no brass,
> Give us our answer and let us pass.

Bang, Bang, Bang!

Groans and maledictions from annoyed adults were all they ever got at our house. But no matter how comfortable I was, or how cold I thought it might be up, I had to rush down and peep out at each troupe in its regalia.

There were usually four or five members to each bunch – boys and girls, not necessarily members of the same family, generally not, in fact. One piece of regalia was compulsory, a bush, festooned with sprigs of holly, shreds of ribbon and coloured paper. 'Ah, they don't do it right at all,' Mam complained once; 'I remember when you'd have to have a wren tied to the bush.' A dead one? 'What else?' her tone seemed to say. 'The lads of the town'd be out all day Christmas Eve hunting them down.' I squirmed. Gay tatters were a lot better.

Naturally all wren-people wore make-up and fancy-dress. Lads with big sisters did best here, sporting cheeks of hectic rouge and cast-off dresses. But the girls were synonymous with cleanliness in my book. And their fathers' shirts, sweat-soiled soft hats and clumpy wellingtons looked good too. Often I didn't recognize who was there, though this is probably less a tribute to wardrobe and make-up than a statement of my own excitement – the daring fun of the participants, the ticklesome knowledge that they were going to get money for riling a townful of sleepy-headed big people.

I wished I was with them. It made me sad and mad to know that the closest I'd get to them was later on when they'd counted their take and told, with relish, how some farmer – John Farrell, perhaps – had not only given them two bob but had sat them down to a fine feed of duck-eggs and hot soda bread.

But not for me, or for any of the heirs of Main Street, the iron-hard, early-morning road, or bright rags under a wintry sky. Besides, what need had we to bring Christmas into the streets? Weren't our own homes good enough for us? Respectability: a door that stayed shut, no matter how clamant the visitors.

2

Yet the lane was part of me, and would have been even if I'd never known an alley or a pauper. This was thanks to Dad, my grandfather; he was born down the lane. The house was just a stone's throw from Swiss Cottage, and fortunately for family pride was the best-kept in the lane; it had yellow ochre trim just like ours. But I'd been told time out of mind that any resemblance between the two dwellings absolutely stopped there. It was all right to come from the lane in Mam's youth (in Mam's youth everything was different), when German bands came oompahing through the town and the Jewish shirt-pedlar went from door to door repeating, 'Von shilling von veek.' 'Ah, God be with old times': that phrase still rings down the years, dragging behind it all its intimidating implications, like a ghost and its chains. People were happy long ago, it implied, and wasn't it the past that put the seal of integrity on all we were and all we should be, and how could you expect God to be with the times that were in it now, with all them Communists and everything.

Looking from my window at Dad's old house and the barn-like structure attached to it which was the family workshop, it intrigued me to think of him as a child looking up at the window and imagining himself Swiss Cottage's proud possessor. Did he need to promise himself a future, and did he see its shape in the high pitch of that roof and the mansard windows, in the very idea of an upstairs? I liked to think so, pleasured in the drift of my own mind by imputing the real drift to his.

I had to imagine, because we never talked, and the bits and scraps about him which I accumulated in the years after his death were less important for their information than for their tone, so that what I have now is not a grandfather but a legend, a genius, an archetype of the great man. All I can picture, however, is a hard-breathing old party with a pepper-and-salt moustache and twinkling eyes who treated me kindly. He'd draw pictures of birds and motorcars in the margin of his *Cork Examiner* while I was waiting to be sent to bed. And he gave me medicine: every day at eleven he'd come home for it, a bottle of porter, mulled. When it was ready he'd take me on his knee and give me some to 'make a man' of me. The closeness of his coarse, sawdust-smelling clothes. The sweet astringency of that warm, aromatic beer sipped from a sugar-coated spoon. I heard the breath whistle through his ravaged tubes; but I only smiled.

Whether or not Dad dreamt of attaining a fine house on Main Street, his rise from the lane has, to me, elements of a dream-journey, or even mythic translation, attached to it, since he had accomplished so much through action and by no other means, while when I thought of my inchoate self, action seemed a perishable option. My father definitely chose not to live on his father's terms, a decision which had the intermit-tent effect of belittling him in my eyes. Whereas, and this is

46

why he struck me as an enlarged presence, Dad was definitely
the son of his father, prehistoric Johnny.

I say prehistoric because, to hear Mam tell it (and, Lord did
I not!), family history began with Dad and herself. She had
good reason to excise any preceeding O'Brien from the record.
But I can't follow her example. Sketchy as my knowledge of it
is, Johnny's is too good a story to obliterate.

Foxy Johnny (he had red hair) hailed from one of those stony
parishes between the east bank of the Blackwater and the sea,
down Aglish way. The native quarter, a place nobody ever
comes from, an area at the far eastern end of which – around
Ring, Old Parish and Helvick Head – people still speak
Irish. Apparently Johnny had sparkling Irish; one of Mam's
few boasts about him was that Brother Geary, one of my
father's teachers, used to come down for advice about idiom
and *blas*. And maybe the old native sang for the teacher, as
well, pouring out, quite unabashed, by the kitchen fire, the
rich, sad love songs of the Decies, his homeland. Sang for my
father too, no doubt (my father loved Irish), and told him
stories, but I can't be sure about that: nothing came down to
me.

Despite Johnny's cultural hoard, however, I don't really see
him as a folklorist's placid accomplice, or even as a remnant of
a vanished race. My sense of him contains a good deal of fire
and drive and hardness. To me he's not a mythic figure just
because he survived, but because he survived in terms he set
for himself: he succeeded.

The odds were daunting. First, he had to learn his trade.
This meant walking the long, lonesome road, bare-footed into
some carpenter in Cappoquin, to whom he served his time –
living-in, probably, which saved his feet but made the
workday longer; getting a taste of the town; setting his face,
gradually but inexorably, against the riverbanks and the
familiar fields which, just then (the 1860s), were coming back
into their own after the famine-ridden forties. I don't know if
his people paid for his apprenticeship, as was the custom
then; if so, I can't imagine how they managed. I've never even
thought about it much, distracted from that aspect of the story
by a more fundamental one which continues to amaze me: his
people's foresight. It's just extraordinary to me that parents,   47

harried virtually to death's door by hunger, would have located the realization of a future (their son's security) in the same landscape. No America for them, and not for their Johnny a life on the land or a life in service, but the life of an independent tradesman: let strength of hand and certainty of eye suffice!

I'm assuming that young Johnny had the strong will of his parents behind him, but of course that's not necessarily so. But it did take an act of will on somebody's part to come into town, and not to be satisfied with Cappoquin, either, but to head for Lismore; where thanks to the Castle, the nobs and toffs were plentiful, and therefore so was work. As Johnny's marriage shows, however, he had will enough to make such moves without anyone's prompting.

His marriage is as unlikely as the rest of his saga. He married Nana. I believe my father was the first to call her that, but I never heard anyone call her anything else. I don't know her name. She was a servant in one of the big houses around Lismore, and was a Northerner, a Protestant, for all I know, an Orangewoman.

What's unlikely is not that she was in service two hundred odd miles from home. In those days, around Lismore at any rate, it was not uncommon for the gentry to hire servants of their own religious persuasion, thinking them more trustworthy, more entitled to have the opportunity of cultivation through service, and a more intimate – not to mention more desirable – embodiment of clean Christian living, than anything the local natives could produce. It was a policy with which Nana, obviously, identified. What she hoped to get out of it, I have no idea: something more, I hope, than the frigid satisfaction of doing her duty. But whatever it was, it's safe to assume, I think, that she never expected to find herself in the arms of that foxy teague, Johnny O'Brien.

How he must have wooed her! Surely nothing less than a mad mindless fling could have brought about a wedding as flagrant as theirs. What else would have made him persist? What else could have made her fly in the face of security and relinquish the keys of her master's meatsafe in favour of a cabinful of kids in Church Lane? I can almost feel the zest of Johnny's satisfaction. Knowing that he'd won that place-proud Northwoman must have made him feel he was going to prosper.

And so he did, working every hour God sent, and fathering a family betimes. No stopping him! Two girls and three boys, and all the boys were brilliant. Jim was the first man in the area to drive a car. Paddy was a miracle-working smith; such a damn shame the 'flu of 1917 took him. And there was George: what couldn't he do?

Mam had the answer to that question: nothing. When the Duchess of Devonshire herself (the Castle! My God; you could rise no higher than to be hired by her) wanted one of her private apartments decorated a special, duck-egg blue, and failed to find the paint either in Cork or London, who mixed it for her? Dad.

Then again: he was out at Colonel Jameson's one time seeing about a job, Mam told me, 'and the girl showed him into the room to wait. When the Colonel came in, he stopped and looked around like there was something odd: "Is that a clock I hear ticking?" says he. "It is, Sir," says Dad. "But that clock hasn't worked for years," said the Colonel. "I'm not surprised," said Dad, "your mantelpiece is out of plumb. I just wound it and put it there on the table." The Colonel nearly dropped,' said Mam, grinning like a girl at such cleverness.

And he saved a man from jail. In those days if your walk wavered by a fraction of an inch a policeman'd be down on you, and you'd be handed thirty days without the option. 'No, but', as Mam went on to explain, 'on top of that, your character was ruined, of course, because no one'd give work to a drunkard.' Anyhow, one Saturday evening Dad was coming up Main Street and just at Ferry Lane corner some fellow from the lane staggered out more or less on top of him. There was an RIC man at the corner, hoping for that very thing. But Dad just caught the drunk by the arm, and held him severely upright the whole length of the street: Dad said he could feel the policeman's eyes looking into his back every step of the way. 'Oh them RIC,' said Mam. 'They were devils. But they got no soot that evening.'

Needless to say, I delighted in those anecdotes – doubly delighted in them, for not only were they marvellous to me in their own right, but the telling of them gave Mam an easeful air of satisfaction and serenity. These are my possessions, said her tone, I am pleased. When she sketched those little scenes, 49 the past was not oppressive. It was like going to the seaside on a weekday, a place with acres of open, idle space, and here a man with balloons, there a beach hut, and along the way a private party under a striped awning.

When I heard of Dad playing the concertina, it was a great relief to find no judgment being made. The memories of his talent as a mimic 'doing to pieces' the flutterings, barks and grufferies of the gentry who were his chief employers, came across as tributes to his independence. And all the time, obsessively, 'Such presence of mind. . . . Great presence of mind.' A tongue that never failed the wit that moved it, a hand that hardly moved less slowly than the eye that prompted it, a man supremely equipped for the life given him to lead, so fitted he must have believed that it was indeed his life, no accident, but an integrated entity. How rare that makes him seem.

None of this (none of what Mam told me, nothing in the pleasurable past) explained how it happened that Dad left the lane and installed himself in the nearest available big house – I wonder, by the way, what he thought of 'cottage' in that house's name: did it strike him that what to him was a mansion, compared to his own home, might to others be a plaything, a dainty architectural frivolity, a picturesque retreat 'from the real world'? I don't suppose he had the luxury or time for thoughts like that (and in any case his mind was too vigorous to dwell on irony). He must have been aware, however, that the house had symbolic value, since he came to it not through making a success of his father's business, but by being so successful in competition. In a word, Swiss Cottage was won in a fight.

Word of the eruption and split never passed Mam's lips, so my sense of what actually took place is hazy. I'd overhear a reference to it, then the following Christmas an obscure piece of information would volley round the dinner table, causing everyone to fall silent for a moment and to look fierce. And then, oddest of all, when I thought about it, there was the situation of Dad's sister, Alice, who lived in perfect normality with her man and children down the street from us. What was odd, though, was that we didn't seem very close to them; at least that was odd to me, because if I had cousins I'd always be down at their house or be having them up to mine. And then, on asking, I was told about Daigue, Alice's husband.

I daresay it was about his name I asked, ever anxiously on the *qui vive* for names stranger than my own. Daigue's name was an abbreviation of its Irish version, Déglán, Declan, the sainted prelate of Foxy Johnny's part of the world, from which Daigue hailed, from which indeed he had been sent into the town of Lismore to serve his time in the work-shop of his successful landsman. And, luckily for him, to marry the boss's daughter. May it not have been that as a result of the fight between Dad and his father, Daigue became heir apparent to the O'Brien family business, causing such a coolness in relations between brother and sister that the next generation would inevitably feel it? So then, it may well have been . . . . And then again, it may not have been that at all, which is what I'd prefer, since there's something devitalizing about making fast, making watertight, a tissue of a plot, as though that were all the past had to offer.

Yet, why was it that when Winny, Dad's other sister, came on a visit from Glasgow – she went there, I presume, because it was the true capital of Nana's kingdom – I had to go down to Alice's to see her; she didn't come next or near our door?

I sat in the overheated parlour, heard what a fine fellow I was turning out to be, and wondered what was that to them. Unfamiliar faces, strange accents, a roaring fire too early in the afternoon. I was given a peach, I remember, a Glasgow peach, for all I knew; another piece of unfamiliarity, oranges being the acme of local fruit treats. And a slobbery job I made of it, juice staining my trousers (*I'll be killed!*), juice congealing on my bare knees. Finished, I held the moist stone in my hand, not knowing how to get rid of it, as embarrassed as if I'd perpetrated some blasphemous *gaffe* or sexual delinquence. And all the time I knew – *I knew* – they were going to make me sing – it was standard practice in those days that when you visited you sung, and you being the child. (They didn't.)

The afternoon was a major piece of evidence that there had been some obscure but decisive explosion in the long ago. Otherwise why would there be strangers with the whimsical, tension-making notion that they and I had some connection? Why, indeed, would there be remote Alice, and the casual 51 cousins, and Daigue with his spectacles as thick as bottle-ends who looked straight through me, wordlessly, as though I was no more to him than a hole in a wall? A whole family, a whole tissue of ties, known indifferently, essentially not known. If that didn't imply an ancient flare-up, what did, I wonder? No doubt I was peculiarly sensitive to gulfs. And then, out of nowhere, people to see me, tender statements, strange fruits. Why? And would they have been strangers to me if there had been no rift?

That afternoon of obscure intentions and unrealistic claims seemed an inscrutable reduction of an unilluminated past (mystery enhanced, not allayed, by fruit and soft talk). This past was what Dad had risen above. He'd detached himself from father, sisters, lane, history, just as he'd secured Mam, a girl of twenty, from Miss O'Shea's workroom, installed her in Main Street (Swiss Cottage, no less), and filled her full of children.

The present was enough for him. That's why he seems so immense to me. He stamped himself on time as emphatically as he stamped his billheads with an inky image of Swiss Cottage. I see in him the drive that will not be detained by 'Why?' I feel from him inklings of understanding that not knowing admits.

3

Church Lane corner, the Mall seat, Ferry Lane corner, the Red House corner, the Monument. As long as it wasn't raining – and often when it was – knots of able-bodied, idle men took their silent ease at these five stations, without even a couple of keys to fiddle with in their noiseless pockets.

If England didn't exist, they would have had to invent it.

But it did exist, a fact of life which made quite a number of these men both happy and sad. Some of them were home from England to convalesce in native air from city life and damp lodgings. They'd be back in Hammersmith before the year was out. Others were home permanently, having tried 'across the pond' (emigration had an argot of its own too, like everything else) a couple of times and baulked at the trauma of it.

I knew one of the latter type fairly well, Cha. He lived in the cabin next door to the house Dad was born in, and where I often visited him, shilling-piece in hand, to have my hair cut. That dwelling was the one in the lane I knew best. It consisted of a hall running about twenty feet from front door to back, with, to the left as you went in, the kitchen, and to the right, two bedrooms. His parents, a brother and sister, originally occupied this space, but only Cha and his sister lived there now.

The kitchen had a table and a couple of chairs in one corner, a dresser with a few pieces of blue delft in another, and in a third, a tripod holding an enamel dish, in which Cha and his sister performed their daily ablutions. There was a larger, low-lintelled open hearth along one wall, with a crane and a few pitch-black, cast-iron utensils hanging from it – the same method of cooking, I noted with amazement, as that used in the depths of the country. (I had a habit of thinking *brusnas* – among other things – more picturesque than necessary. It unnerved me to find I was wrong.) Above the fireplace, a mirror, two-foot square, thick varnished frame, and stuck in its bottom left-hand corner, a picture.

Kneeling on a chair with a pillow-case around my neck while Cha clipped – I can still see him lifting the gleaming chrome shears out of its oiled-paper nest, as good as the day he'd bought it (but what moved him to buy it?) – I had plenty of time to study that picture. It was of Cha at a dance, a wonderfully pretty girl in his arms (in my memory she wears a white dress). In the shadows, other couples are having a large time, but nothing can possibly surpass the radiance of Cha's expression.

The picture, he tells me, was taken in England. I know it must be somewhere other than Lismore because its brightness and frank joy is in such contrast to the bleak space it now looks out on. I ask him why he didn't stay in England, and receive various answers: the work is slavery; Birmingham is a woeful dump – not a tree or a river in it, just smoke and dirt; 'I couldn't stick it, boy.' He'd rather be at home, working when he could, ambling from one corner to another when he   53 couldn't, drinking like a fish all the time. He was about thirty. Already his lips were drawing into a pinch, his jaws were hollowing, his eyes were losing their lustre. He'd probably had his finest hour, was lucky to have a photo commemorating it. And there were dozens like him, in whose long faces and sagging, corner-influenced shoulders I saw that poverty was only partly a financial matter.

It wasn't until years later, however, after I'd taken the Rosslare boat myself and worked and drank in Cricklewood and Paddington and Camberwell Green that I got some sense of how London could turn old neighbours into casualties. When I was a child, it wasn't sympathy I learned to offer them, but reproof. They were failures, I heard; they couldn't stick it over there and they couldn't settle down decent at home. They were corner-boys. ('Don't put your hands in your pockets,' I was admonished; 'you'll end up like one of them Sheridans.') They were drunkards; all they lived for was rolling home legless, stinko, senseless, lousy, blotto, blind and stocious, singing in voices that seemed to emerge from cavernous bottles, keeping decent people awake, pissing in the gutter – shameless tramps!

And to make matters worse, in the eyes of my loved ones, this kind of low, blackguarding carry-on, was very often subsidized by their tougher-minded brethren who had managed to stick it out 'over', and who came home for their fortnight's holiday with more money than sense, decked out in the fake finery of Fifty-shilling Tailors. They, in a sense, were worse for having succeeded, or so I inferred from Swiss Cottage kitchen critiques. Born to nothing, just like those who sponged off them, how could they have got on by the strength of their arms alone in a place where nothing thrived except smoke and godlessness? Well, of course, there was only one answer: what little moral fibre they had must have simply collapsed. Mind you, they were hardly Irish anyhow, to begin with (meaning they existed in ideological innocence, their allegedly offensive occasions immune from considerations of Church and State), so . . . . And the accents of them; honestly you'd swear it was a tin can being kicked around! Oh, and did you see the one that Kip Tobin has home with him – my God, talk about a masterpiece in oils! The adult urchins whom England had unnerved may not have had a ha'penny to scratch themselves with, but at least they didn't stoop *that* low. They'd remained elements of a recognizable world, where neither flesh nor devil found a footing. They were the poor who, as the Master promised, we'd have always with us. Demoralization was accepted as part of this plan, but fancy clobber was vanity of vanities . . . .

The thing to do really, the honourable and admirable way of dealing with the unfortunate necessity of England, was to go there and not change. Few indeed there were with the strength of character to do so, but thank God we had our own Lizzie as an example. That she was still 'natural', had no accent, dressed as a mirror of sober sense, came to us unencumbered by lover or even close friend, amounted to a body of law, from which judgments on those of more friable backbone could be drawn.

And it wasn't that Elizabeth had a soft job either, or was protected from the vicissitudes and temptations of an alien civilization. On the contrary, as a nurse, she was as exposed as anyone. Meal after meal, she dawdled over tea and cigarettes and told us the worst – vignettes from the children's wards, how Mr Evans had finally pulled through, the policeman who'd shot himself – grey brain weeping from his temple, 'and when they brought him in he was still alive!' And still Lizzie went to mass, went walking with her old pal Nora Willoughby, stayed in at night knitting. 'You'd swear she's never been a day away.' The refrain of friendly neighbours, the greatest compliment an emigrant could be paid. To journey unscathed. To remain true. Exile as a myth of stasis. Emigration as fidelity's enriching rite.

Elizabeth certainly had the air of a notary about her. She was terse, she was stern, she could be as scratchy as a starched uniform. She was thin, worn to the bone by nights of painful moaning and days of fighting her corner, the latter in defence of her professional judgment and her nationality. Woe betide anyone attempting to impugn either! Long stories recalling in detail the criticisms rebutted and the slurs denied stiffened our spines with every telling. They all concluded satisfactorily: 'I gave *them* their answer.' The colour would leave her face, then, and she'd reach for her Players. We all felt proud of her, but the stories unnerved us: they served to say, how distressing to be necessary to 'the English' (trans., the alien world) 55 yet to be made feel unwanted at the same time. And we all thought, well aren't we better off here at home, after all?

Elizabeth, however, did not necessarily agree with that sentiment, and felt very irritated by the dead-and-alive character of Irish life. After a day or two at home she'd begin to get restless and would offer to wash down walls or dig the garden, requiring some light diversion of that kind to maintain her familiar output of energy. If some such outlet was not forthcoming she could get rather aggressive about the state of the country, and sometimes even about the attitudes of her nearest and dearest. I remember one hell of a political row in the course of which she called us all Communists, and scourged us verbally like a proper Dante Riordan. More Irish than the Irish themselves . . . . But I was afraid of her in those moods. I admired her guts, her tenacity, her utter belief in her own position. She had to be that way, I reasoned, to endure England. I just hated having to shake in my shoes because of it.

It was only in Elizabeth that I encountered such singleness. Other grown-ups home from England – men, respectable denizens of Main Street – never showed such fierce integrity. In them, there always seemed something blurred or softened, some minor addition to their original selves, a tiepin featuring the logo of London Transport, a trick of accent (Peadar Hickey used to say, 'How are *you*?' – his accent Lismore through and through, his emphasis pure Peckham Rye).

For men did go to England from Main Street. Emigration was never the prerogative of the lane, any more than it was that of the provinces, though it surprised me quite a bit to discover that Dubliners also crossed the water. Girls from Main Street also went, of course, girls like Chrissy and Elizabeth, exasperated finally by the nullity of home, striking out for independence with their twenties half-over, often never to be seen again. But it's the men I remember best, since their departure left their children in a state somewhat similar to my own, and I felt less unusual for a time, until the Daddy came back again for good or the whole family went to join him.

I remember one of my pals and his holidaying Da inviting me to go with them as they passed on a walk out the Deerpark Road. I accepted with pleasure, and a certain amount of excitement. Since talk at home more often had Main Street doings as its focus, rather than the lane or other paupers' quarters. I had a much more developed sense of the newsworthiness and novelty of Bill Egan's return. But I was sorry afterwards. Instead of hearing about bright lights and smart living in the great metropolis, as I thought I might from someone not related to me (my own people declining to for fear, I suppose, they'd feel guilty later for colouring my impressionable mind), Bill junior and I were treated to an avalanche of invective.

Never in all my listening days to lane-talk – and I listened to it close and long – had I heard such language; never had suspected that the father of a friend of mine, a man whom I myself knew to own a suit before he went to England, would curse and swear with such fluency and invention. And in front of children too! My own father, who was anything but square, spoke to me sharply when, in all innocence, I called one of the local mongrels a 'hoor', a term borrowed from Bocky Ford. Now here was Bill Egan scorching the ears off us with his terrible tongue.

He cursed the town and a lot of people in it; they were so stingy, he said, 'they wouldn't give their shit to the crows'. He denounced the countryside and all belonging to it, including not so veiled references to his wife's people. When we came to the cabins by the railway-gates, he fucked from a height the state of the country. 'God Christ Almighty!' he cried (a novel formulation to me, and I nearly laughed). Priests, brothers, and nuns came under the lash, everything and anything. The world consisted of cunts and fuckan eejits.

I never said anything about it, either at home or to my pal Billy. The whole performance was too amazing and too embarrassing to complain about. And of course I'd no idea what prompted it, apart from a vague sense that being forced to leave hearth, home and loved ones for icy digs in Kensal Rise must be a bitter pill to swallow. Next time I met him, though adult, Bill was, as the local expression has it, 'as game as paint', if anything, extra-jolly. I never happened onto his bitterness again, but that surprises me less than that one cloudburst of it when all we were doing was out walking, an activity that I'd hitherto understood adults to practise for the sake of their youngsters, not the other way around.

Compared to Mr Egan's shower of bile and Elizabeth's armour-plated defences, Church Lane's English contingent, so glibly condemned for their foolery, were the soul of harmlessness and honest-to-God good fun. The gaudy clothes, the speech dented by Cockney, the boastful street-corner bombast about drink and women (mostly, and more feelingly, about drink), seem now merely flesh wounds in the war of nerves in which every emigrant serves. Style and manner – some people even came home with new walks, rapid city struts; not always confined to girls in impossible (and surely sinful!) stiletto heels, either – were understandable blemishes, predictable deformities, tolerable insignia of altered lives.

Of course, they were 'shoving on', 'shaping', 'trying to cut a dash'. Why not? Even then, as I took in the criticism, I didn't see what fuelled it. I found myself more naturally drawn to the know-nothing exuberance of the temporarily returned, their longing to make a splash, their cultural anarchy. And this was only partly because I detested the asperity of our kitchen council, not for its lack of charity, since I had no moral self-consciousness then, but because its atmosphere made me feel intimidated, fearful, frail.

Besides, why shouldn't they have their holiday, their hullabaloo? Why shouldn't they feel cocky, now that they'd paid off the family debt to the town's hucksters? Everyone could eat sweet-cake now for a fortnight and real rashers too, not the customary handful of scraps from the bacon-slicer. Gin-and-limes could be consumed too, by the bucketful if needs be, though all the stay-at-home world would dispute its claim to be a proper drink. And, long after midnight, let the street resound to the cracked tenors and 'Hear my song, Violetta!'

If there was a deliberate undertow of *épater* to such carousing, so much the better, I thought. Because in one respect I knew Mam's criticisms to be true (Mam, source and inspiration of Swiss Cottage class-consciousness): these show-off visitors were nobodies. As soon as they turned Parks Road corner, making for the station with their flat, cardboard suitcases, they effectively resumed their anonymous lives: their hand-callousing, noisy, repetitive lives; their dirty, lonesome, well-paid lives. So weren't they right to act like somebodies when they could?

That's what the lane gave me, anyhow; a view of double-ness. I saw it in the place itself, in its active nullity, in the chronic incompleteness of poverty's finality. It was in my playmates too, in the uneven equilibrium between handball and hunger, debt and devilment that their lives represented. I learned that their lives were hectic, but its joy brittle. I learned that going out for the wren was a great gas, but that as sure as Confirmation or First Communion time came round, the same youngsters, just about as unrecognizable now in new clothes, would come knocking at our door again with, 'Me mother said you wanted to see me.' Only this time to meet with success; 'Oh, I do, child, sure aren't you looking lovely – here, now.' Silver coin pressed into pale, moist palm, immediate flight of recipient. (The new outfit had to be paid for somehow.)

With this abundance of otherness I freely identified, a glad act of psychic disobedience. And as for those gin-swilling, vowel-devouring peacocks in their British chain-store plumage, they became my archetypes of doubleness, embodiments of home's foreignness and the allure of the far away, specialists in longing and in longing mollified. Welcome aliens. Metropolitans. Brothers to whom in doubleness I felt my own life obscurely but enlargingly twinned.

III

THE DUCHY

1

'Picturesquely pitched on the banks of the Blackwater – ' Pat Lyons read, and there Brother Blake interrupted him: '"Picturesquely *pitched* . . . . " Well, sure that sounds like someone threw it there. You should say "picturesquely situated".'

Unabashed, Pat resumed. He was reading out his composition on Lismore Castle to the whole class. Blakey had asked him to. It had come first. I listened dully, alert only when the interruption came, though it was nowhere near admonishing enough to please me. I was mortified and cross. My effort had only come third.

I was upset because family, as well as personal, pride had been offended. The assignment excited me because it was so different from the usual 'A Wet Day' or 'A Bicycle Wheel Tells Its Own Story': it was a much more agreeable challenge to write about something substantial, familiar and famous. But I hadn't expected the grown-ups at home to join in. Usually they left me severely alone with my homework. Now, however, the novel opportunity arose to say something about the most dominant physical feature of their world. The Castle – Irish seat of the Duke of Devonshire – was the structure which denoted that the village belonged to a context larger than its own. Yet much as that belonging was cherished, the manner of it was hopelessly beyond the village's control. Everything connected with the Castle, besides the emotions it evinced, was pre-ordained, possessed, arbitrated over by 'others': nobles, superiors, employers. The Duke's dominion was a perfect and apparently indestructible embodiment of the soul of ownership: the dispossessed admiring the proprietor's fortress, the fleeced kissing the shears. I admired, too, not feeling particularly dispossessed. And so did Chrissy.

With an air of authority which clearly pleased her, she dictated, 'Built by King John in 1185 . . . ' and I bowed my head over the spotless copybook.

Assured by Chrissy's enthusiasm that this was going to be my finest literary hour to date, I was extremely concerned that the composition be a masterpiece of penmanship as well. Of all the attainments of primary school, the one I took most pride in was 'light writing'; script faint to the point of virtual illegibility, barely more prominent than the blankness of the paper it rested on, a film of whose perspiration it might be imagined to be: testament, in its fastidiousness, to superb nib control and delicacy of finger pressure! No easy accomplishment, given the equipment: the coarse, absorbent texture of the off-white, brown-flecked jotters, the wooden-shafted pen with a nib the size of a cockroach, and just as resistant to being toilet-trained, and school ink which came in powder form and had to be mixed; it evaporated leaving a sticky sludge at the bottom of the ceramic inkwells. Against such odds I pitted myself, anxious to acquire a skill which had, I perceived, overtones of decorum, care and ceremonial attention, a translation of colouring-book *politesse*.

There was a further not unimportant consideration. Over and above the satisfaction of calligraphic heroics for their own sake, a blot-free copybook could mean a slap-free start to the school day. At the very least it would spare me Blakey's jibes about how we shouldn't be trying to plant a row of turnips with our pens, though God knows maybe some of us'd be better off trucking in mud and dirt, because we just weren't able to tell A from B, and never would. 'So come out here.' Then would follow a list of names, a scraping of reluctant hobnailed boots as the victims advanced, the production of the length of seasoned ash. And *swish, swish*: four blows apiece. The tension, the moaning, the lads with their incompetent hands thrust under armpits and between knees, faces gargoyled to ward off tears, every ounce of their presence bent in wringing out the detestable ashen sting, the exposure, the affront.

'Third!' exclaimed Chrissy and Mam together, taken mightly aback. 'Who came first?' and when I told them, 'Humph!' ironically, as though detecting a design, 'Who got second?'

64   'John O'Connor.'

'Oh my God!' This surprised them so much that they had to turn to insults. 'John Butch, h'mm? Oul Mallet-skull . . . ?' Then, this attack of bile subsiding, 'What did he say?' (Blake, about mine).

'Too much history. He said I got it all out of a book.'

'Blasted cheek: does he take us for a parcel of know-nothings? What was Pat Lyons's like?'

I mentioned his alliterative indiscretion.

'Ha, picturesquely pitched, I'm sure. Where did he get that kind of language? Don't mind, boy; you're better than the whole lot of them put together.'

By this time I hardly minded at all, certainly not half as much as my elders and betters, with their mutterings about favouritism and mumbled explanations of how this blatant slight had come about. But Mam and Chrissy wouldn't rest until they'd arrived at a plausible salve for wounded self-respect. To do so was a sophisticated exercise in the hermeneutics of community attachments, requiring considerable imaginative and forensic skill, allowing intuition free play, invoking precedent and provenance and eking every last ounce of potential significance from the commonplace, until at length, slaked and satisfied by their thoroughness, they had nothing more to say but, 'That's it, surely.'

'Oh, that's it, now.'

Secure interpretation of the everyday was a must, so little else tolerated or responded to interpretation.

Perhaps one reason that Chrissy and Mam vented their frustration so vehemently was that they'd never expected an opportunity to express themselves formally about the Castle. To be sure, the form was adventitious, unforeseen, but at least they knew they were equal to its demands (more than equal, indeed, as Brother Blake's criticism pointed out). Maybe they thought my failure to come first a judgment on what they expressed. Or was it simply that, irrespective of the approach, the Castle maintained its distance from common life and thereby, passively and inscrutably, upheld its identity as an enigma – impenetrable, unapproachable, remote? It simply stood in our midst as an irreproachable monument to land, money, grandeur, supremacy and all the other trappings of Mammon, which were not for the likes of us (whose kingdom was not of this world). And yet, for all its difference, we thought there was something of 'our own' about it, we extended to it a secret sympathy, an illicit intimacy, as though in spite of all appearances, we understood it. Tacitly, though without embarrassment, we gave the symbol psychic house-room (How could we not? Wasn't it a fact of life?); we domesticated the enigma, thereby making it enigmatic indeed – teasing, taunting, ticklesome. If Waterford City was known as *urbs intacta* (never penetrated by siege), what variety of virginity might describe our situation? Certainly some loftier, purer classification: perhaps we were the Holy Innocents, sanctified by our elimination from history, limbo's founding dynasty.

We were proud of our intimacy, but it was an intimacy with what lay beyond us, and we remained unrequited. So our pride was without hope. Our history – that chain of events in the first twenty years of this century which we could definitely call our own – discounted all the Castle stood for, yet had not installed in our awareness anything like so powerful or secular a symbol as the Castle. Nationalism's spiritual picturesqueness was no match, on a day-to-day basis, with scenic ditto. Every time the Duke's standard – a corkscrew of green snake on a lime field – was raised, the victory of the Republic seemed more like the triumph of party instead of people, since we in Lismore were still attached to a remoteness; we were still experiencing decentredness of a sort, surrounded by a code of cordons and warnings to trespassers, involved in a species of psychological absenteeism. And not only psychological, either; the Duke was still the great landlord.

It even looked as if the Castle had its back to the town, because all we could see was the façade that fronted the river, the apartments contemplating the deep woods and haunches of mountain which it held in fee, averse to where we lived. The river was alive with salmon and trout, but not everyone could fish for them. Permission had to be sought 'from the office' (trans., from the bailiff) and very few could afford the permit or the tackle. All most locals had was the time to fish, not the material wherewithal. But a certain amount of poaching went on, especially downriver where lived a family bearing an Irish nickname, the Garabhánachs ('the coarse ones'). Blackwater *mafiosi*, masters of the night, dare-devils. Even on our highly respectable table a whole salmon would sometimes appear, payment for a funeral perhaps. At those dinners we would have rare silence, and savour, along with the delicate flesh (the colour and softness of mild twilight), the unfamiliar juices released by wrong-doing. It was like eating royalty.

Since everything about the Castle except its physical presence seemed tainted by abstractions, I suppose I shouldn't be surprised to find my knowledge of it so slight. But I am. Did I repress my curiosity about it in order to keep the reality of its 'difference' intact? Or did I just shun it, thinking that since the way of life it represented was not for the likes of me I would make a virtue of my disenfranchisement and seek a way of life that was?

Of course I know a certain amount about its history, but I know nothing at all about its life. I know that it has three hundred and sixty-five windows. . . . But is that true, really? I think not, now. I think that's just an example of the myth of the everyday which the Castle inspired, its presence attributing to the most trivial detail the possibility of being part of a system. A window is a purpose, an integer of vision. We lived in the duchy of synecdoche.

One good thing the Castle did, though: it gave work. There was the Castle farm, the sawmill, the hatchery where the salmon fry were incubated, and there were wood-rangers and water-bailiffs as well. I make no mention of the office, where rents were paid and complaints lodged. Two Protestants supervised it, one of them our neighbour, Mr Copley, the other a man by the name of Arthur King, remarkable to childish me, not for his name but for his car, a baby Fiat, which looked like the shell of a snail.

Yet even though the Castle's range of activities made it a going concern, and certainly diminished its picturesque properties for those employed there, still there seemed to be an elusive quality in its enterprise. It was as though the products of the work were not translated into the life of the town. And so even approaching the Castle from a practical standpoint it was still quite difficult for me to ascertain what really went on there. 'Lismore Castle is a Private Residence' a big sign proclaimed. It was simply beyond the bounds of possibility to enter one of its rooms, to sit on a seat, to breathe its atmosphere. The grounds were opened once a year for a garden fête to support the Jubilee Nurses Fund and Mam and

Chrissy delighted in examining the splendid hydrangeas and immaculate herbaceous borders, handiwork of Dave Montgomery, the Northern gardener. Otherwise, the only reason to venture within the Castle purlieu was business, purely business.

It may have been that its employees confused me, but I sensed most palpably the invisibility of Castle life because there seemed to be elements of ghostliness about them. John Noel Pollard was a butler there, and sometimes even (I heard it proudly said) went home to Chatsworth with His Grace. Morning and evening when the Duke was in residence one saw a glimpse of mackintosh, dickey and bow-tie gliding down Chapel Street to work. A quiet man, soul of discretion, a shadow of high living, a walking borderline.

There was the man called Pad the Bishop, a sawyer, dressed perpetually in black, with black eyes as deep-set and as fixed as rivets or as knots in oak, black-avis'd too, hefty mutton-chop whiskers unshorn, his face otherwise brownish, as though porter-soaked. He never said hello to anyone. He was too forbidding a sight even for us kids to shout after.

And there was Moss, Mam's brother, my friend, my mentor in melancholia, to whom a three-volume study would hardly begin to do justice, about the sorrow of whose life it is so difficult to speak. Pad the Bishop's colleague. Who lost the use of his left hand in that same sawmill – disguising the fact, and at the same time drawing attention to it, by always wearing a thumbless black glove. Who'd show me the scar sometimes, if I nagged him to: unnatural, metallic brightness of skin, wizened, hamstrung tendons. Who was just about deaf from the saws' callous singing. Whose voice was as low and slow-moving as a salmon in sunshine. He asked for nothing, refused nothing, married nothing, sired nothing. A true exile, standing at the Red House corner with his cronies in the evenings. He'd drink if it was offered, not otherwise. He'd smoke a pipe, go to Rosary. Placid to the point of anaesthesia, stoical as a boulder. Desire's enemy. Less ghost than ruin . . . Beckett-fodder. That the current of life should run so unobtrusively, so inexpressively, and still be truly life . . . .

The superiors were strange, too; but no doubt they were supposed to be, at least it was expected that they avail of the

latitude which history and fortune had bestowed on them.
Prilaux certainly did, but that wasn't thought strange, at least
not to begin with. His behaviour conformed to a model of
acceptability which was lost on me, but which I was unable to
criticize seeing as how Mam approved of it ('Isn't he a fine
figure of a young fella?') and Chrissy was captivated by his
crinkly curls and his candid handsome face. None of the leath-
ery labouring farmer about him – and I believe I heard in the
women's tone, 'Thank God! At last, a gent, a swell, a toff . . . .'

I don't know exactly what Prilaux did. Steward, agent,
overseer, under-secretary: the realms of influence and tiers of
attainment were something I could only imagine. Besides,
what mattered was his visibility. 'Morning. Fine day!' he
klaxoned in his strangled, educated accent, trotting through
the town on his immense chestnut hunter. Now that was class!
In a series of delightfully casual gestures he'd dismount, tether
the beast to a lamp-post and stroll into the Co-op. 'Morrow,
Pat; say, be a good fellow . . . .' You could hear him all over the
street. But what cared he who knew his business? His voice
spoke of his station: powerful, tactless, carefree. And then one
day he was gone – cavalry twill, ruddy complexion, chestnut
mare and all. Where? 'Up the country, somewhere,' spoken
resentfully, because nobody had any real means of knowing;
because everybody found now that they didn't know Mr
Prilaux at all. 'Must've got a better offer . . . .' Silence. Incredul-
ity.

Mr Copley vanished too, which struck me as even stranger.
He more or less lived with us, sure. And he wasn't young, he
was a 'nice, natural being', in his middle-years now a book-
keeper, a bachelor, as mild as a clergyman, as kindhearted a
neighbour as anyone could want – a lot better than one of our
own crowd, whom in modesty and friendliness he sought to
resemble. Plus, were more proof needed of his amiable heart,
Mam repeated over and over how he would exclaim, seeing
her dressed for the chapel, 'Oh isn't it fine for you!' He lived
next door, and Minnie Foley with the whiskers was his cook
and char.

No throwback he. Mr Copley was no hussar *manqué*, had no
equine leanings, didn't in any way suggest those social
archetypes of Anglo-Ireland, the buck, the youngest son, the
feckless student, the subaltern, all of whom were evident in

Prilaux's make-up (which is probably why the town took to him; not only was he lively, he was recognizable). But few knew Mr Copley, who kept himself to himself, like a decent Christian. Only why in the name of goodness would someone as unencumbered as he, as self-effacing, as assimilated to the no-horse town, want to do anything to himself? It was a great shock when he did, however: we realized that there must have been a Mr Copley there that nobody saw. I wasn't told what happened, but I remember screening myself behind adult skirts and listening. 'Razor . . . bath water . . . police,' I heard. And I saw Mr Copley no more.

In view of such all-pervading poor visibility, it was no surprise to us that the Duke and all belonging to him had no presence, no vitality, no immediacy as far as we were concerned. We didn't expect him to impinge on us as a human being. Distance was ingrained in us. No doubt he and his retinue drove out in the shooting-break to inspect the far-flung estate, to bag pheasants, to condescend to their British brethren, whose homes and farms occupied all that fertile valley. Moss and the men of his time doffed their caps as he passed. But I didn't know him from Adam. Or his guests either, which occasionally proved frustrating. President Kennedy's sister, Kathleen, came to stay and 'insisted' (Mam proudly claimed) on walking up to early Sunday mass with the skivvies from the kitchen. The whole town was frustrated when Fred Astaire was one of the guests at the house-party. We could hardly contain ourselves. Aristocracy bedamned! Here was one of the new, more uplifting élite, someone to whom self-advertisement was, we believed, second-nature. So surely we'd catch a glimpse of him, latch on to the twentieth-century if only by the strength of an eye-lash, snap out of our familiar feudal shuffle and hit the high-spots, just for an instant, with the Tzar of Terpsichore! There was hardly a man, woman or child in the town who didn't, privately, surreptitiously, obsessively think of themselves as Ginger Rogers – speaking of whom, by J., she must be Irish; where else would she get that hair?

But sight or sound of Fred we never saw. What did we expect, though, really – that he climb to the top of the flag-tower and give an exhibition, the taps amplified for the edification of the whole countryside, thereby proving his bodily existence while ensuring that he kept his distance? I don't know. What right had we to expect anything? The more daring spirits of the town – Chrissy, for one – said when the visit was over that it was a shame that the Duke didn't think of having a dance in his guest's honour. But the Duke wasn't that sort: private was as private did. And Fred remained in privacy as well, a rumour of a person, image only; in our eyes, all his being concentrated in the unique form of a celluloid dervish. Still – we attempted not to feel offended – sure how could you not take to a fellow by the name of Fred; such a candid, manly kind of a name . . . . At the same time, it was a shame, we agreed, that given the Duke's resources, all he could think of in the way of diversion for the town was the garden fête. Didn't he know as well as we did that the town was out on its feet, that compared to our state, the paralysis of Joyce's Dublin was a veritable St Vitus's dance? I don't know. But divil a Ritz did the Duke encourage us to put on.

Here again, however, consistency was not the rule – mercifully, since inconsistency at least kept the state of things lifelike. The Duke did offer one notable stimulus to our cultural edification. Whether this was what he had in mind, I have no way of knowing. I would guess not, though, since if it was it would mean that His Grace could hardly avoid the benevolently satirical aspect of his gesture. And he was born to a condition which immunized him from such game-playing. Besides, he was only a plain man doing his duty. Selfless, in his way. (And, as I keep wanting to say, invisible.)

His contribution to the mind of Lismore consisted of no less than that Prince of the Turf, Royal Tan, whom the Duke purchased not long after his triumph in the Grand National and whom he retired to the lush grazing of County Waterford for an old age of ease and admiration. The town was jubilant – we'd been noticed! We were in the papers! Royal Tan was used to such attention; we were not. Everyone went to pay their respects to our famous guest, delighted to have such a celebrated athlete to talk about, with whose exploits we could all identify, a star we could understand as though he were one of ourselves. And visible, too.

He arrived late in the year, October, I think. We'd go over to see him after school. He had a paddock to himself behind

Dunne's cottage, and stayed at the far end of it, by the gate, a brown statue in the dank autumn air. We couldn't get close to him without wrecking our jackets, so we peeped over the brambles and waited for him to do something unprompted. He never did. Sometimes a couple of old-timers would come by to pay their visit. They'd stand apart from us, murmuring, reviewing the great stayer's career, caps pushed well back the better to scratch heads in amazement, envisaging the air full of divots and jockey's curses, fortunes changing hands, honour redounding and glory reflected – then, at last, sidling reluctantly away, unable to see more, and a final murmur: 'Wisha, God bless him, anyhow . . . . '

2

The Castle was the Duchy's centrepiece, of course, but up and down the valley, from Fermoy (fifteen miles west) to the sea at Youghal (fifteen miles south) there were establishments with mores and appurtenances just as difficult for me to visualize. Homes of the gentry: Glencairn, Salterbridge, Ballinwillin, Tourin, Dromana, Headborough . . . . Each within sight of the other (each its neighbour's sentry), but snug behind screens of beech and removed from the common thoroughfare by shady driveways, choosing custodianship of the slow, black, powerful river over the fellowship of the road.

No doubt it wasn't necessarily the case that these demesnes were deliberately installed as Castle satellites. It looked that way, though, all the more so since those who owned them had, with one or two outstanding exceptions (the Villiers-Stuarts of Dromana, for example), little or no truck with valley life. They were people who'd retired from imperial service and now were gentle-folk, meaning, as far as I could see, that they did nothing. Lilies of the field they were, neither siring children, nor tilling land, nor like the town's beached souls, making their peace with God. They seemed to have found in our valley simply a place to be, a place to wait out their time. Accustomed to being abroad all their active lives, they retained the vestige of that condition to the end, just as they retained 'Major' and 'Captain'. Only now they served in the temperate zone and in a comatose district – inexpensive too; lusher and (being unfamiliar) less changed than the green and pleasant acres of their youth. Cultural refugees sharing a secret, shameful kinship with the men of no property whose labour they needed but whose existence they shunned. Yet still they stood to attention by the stately river, as though expecting the royal barge of another *Fidei Defensor* to appear, as though they had not been evacuated by history.

We knew them, a little; the family did, I mean. Mam knew them best, of course, had seen them in their Edwardian hey-day. And she would have made it her business to know them in any case, being insatiable in her study of genealogy and the ways of rich-folk (perusing the *Sunday Express* for the latest doings of Billy Wallace . . .). She was able to think of these types as people. No wonder: Hadn't she and Dad danced the night away at Shane Jameson's twenty-first birthday party? The car was sent in for them. Dad let down any amount of whiskey, but it only made him dance the more. My eyes shone, listening, but not as brightly as hers, remembering.

Georgie generally had less contact with the gentry than Dad had. There were fewer gentry, of course. And I think the old guard looked very slightly askance at him, as though wondering if he *quite* had his father's winning combination of Edwardian *savoir faire* and Yankee know-how. Well, he didn't *quite*, because he was living in a world that didn't ask enough of him, a world in which it was impossible, and worse still, seemed irrelevant, to make the kind of break-through that his powerful forebears had.

Nevertheless, George could impress in his own way. Mam was fond of telling of how when he was working at Maxwell's, some woman, a guest, a writer, engaged him in spirited conversation about matters historical and professed herself, according to one of the hands who afterwards told Mam, to be most impressed by Geo's wide learning and sharp analyses. Forty years after Anglo-Ireland's swansong, Mam was not at all critical of the swanky guest's apparent surprise that a workman knew anything other than a few prayers and quaint phrases. She was too busy being proud of Georgie and pointing the lesson to me (*Read!*) to think like that.

It's also tempting to believe that Mam's critical powers were temporarily suspended because she needed to concentrate on organizing the story. The story seemed organized because of the air of composure and instruction which attended its telling. Mam didn't quite raise an index finger or stand forth as though sermonizing on a mount. But all that was there in the measured tone, the pauses, the teller's steady eye.

Not all Mam's stories were accompanied by these effects. But the one about being taken out to see Dromana by Mr Gorringe, the agent, was. And so were the tales of Chef and Madame (pronounced 'Madam' by Mam), a French couple, members of the Duke's entourage. Perhaps it was from them that she got the word which I never heard anyone else use – *cadet*, employed pejoratively as a verb as well as noun. So-and-so (from the lane, inevitably) was a useless *cadet*; he should be earning a living, not *cadeting* around. It means to idle, to affect gutter dandyism, to sponge drink. (For more, see Lenehan in Joyce's 'Two Gallants'.)

Other than that, which may well be totally wrong, I have no idea of what Chef and Madame said or did, which annoys me, as it's another door shut against my entering Castle life. All I remember is Mam's tone. But that's memory: if it were complete it would be difficult to contain, and redundant to exercise. And the tone is something. It gave the sense that what was being recounted was special. It lent the material wholeness, lifted it out of the common run of talk. I wasn't always able to appreciate the specialness because it seemed to have something to do with the influence and presence of the gentry, of which I had no direct experience. So I couldn't quite *see*, always . . . . Not that I minded: the stories' component of invisibility made them much more interesting – family folktales instead of history, parables instead of home truths.

It must have suited me to keep the gentry at a distance. I say this because I find it hard to believe now, that when I got my own bike – Georgie (of course) bought it for me from Simon Chute, Colonel Foster's grandnephew – and was able to visit any big house I wanted, I just didn't bother; I whizzed past their tall, green, frozen-looking gates without a second thought. Joe McDokes and The Three Stooges were what occupied my imagination, not colonization: my only ache was for a full present; the past was an accident, just one of those things.

And cycling was glorious, it brought me to enough places where I'd never been to make me not miss tentatively pedalling up lime-guarded avenues to places where I wasn't wanted. It wasn't just me either: we all learned to ride at the same time – Peter Hickey (who taught me), John O'Connor, Liam Murphy, Tommy Heffernan, Paddy Farrell. In those days traffic was so light – nothing apart from horse and donkey carts and an odd bus or creamery lorry – that we could freewheel with impunity, three abreast, arms across each others shoulders . . . . Flying down the Sweep, Bottle Hill, Corbett's Hill, the Kennel Heights. Never before was the mind so sated by the body's power, never since has air been so fresh and sweet.

We went to where the river Bride nuzzled swampily into the Blackwater, and tried to slither out to where the poachers' black skiffs lay up-ended on mud flats, beetles basking before nightwork stirred them again. We went to Kilahalla to the ship. A real ship, its appearance possible because the river was tidal as far inland as Cappoquin. A dirty old Dutch coaster, the *De Wadden* of Rotterdam, but wonderfully mysterious to us. We were in school when it carried on its business of loading pit-props for South Wales, so whenever we visited it silence and idleness wrapped it all around: spectral, gull-grey emissary from beyond the sea. Typically enough, it stood too far out in the water for us to get on board. But looking had its own satisfaction: it was something to see foreignness. What we didn't see, the big houses, we didn't care about. We sped through the whole of that land with never the slightest thought to who owned it. Any such consideration would have struck us as a massive irrelevance, for what bearing could it possibly have on the freedom of the road?

So removed were the gentry from us that it was almost possible to pretend they didn't exist, even on the day of the races, the Lismore point-to-point, their festival. The races were another mark of Lismore's distinctiveness; it was the only meeting within a fifteen-mile radius of the town. But it wasn't that so much that we kids were glad of, but the fact that we got the day off school and the knowledge that the whole town 75 would be infected with a kind of Church Lane looseness.

Race day was usually around the start of spring ploughing, and in addition to Maiden Plates and Selling Handicaps had all kinds of peripheral novelties. A one-legged young man, with his head to one side like Christ in our oleographs, sat in the bushes by the gate and plucked his banjo lackadaisically. The man who lay on his bare back amid broken bottles came every year, and sometimes bent an iron bar over his upper arm for good measure. We watched his tattoos flinch in the intense torque of his muscles, and wondered if he'd learned the knack of bending in the Navy. The tattoos were so deep-dyed, so blue, it was as though the sea had imbued the strong man with something of itself.

There were stalls selling gaudy trinkets, and a marquee dispensing Murphy's stout, and there were swingboats containing little girls with bows in their hair clutching the white plastic handbags which were all they could still use from their First Communion trousseaus, and – uuUp went the boat! – puking all over their petulant Daddies.

The fortune-teller was there too, and around her tiny tent there was a vague group of men and women trying to look casual and not like a queue, but casting tense glances at each other to intimidate any prospective place-poachers. They appeared furtive not just becuse they were nervous about what awaited them within, not even because they were afraid some neighbour would see them and deride their longing, but because going to a fortune-teller was a sin. It broke, I think, the first commandment: 'I am the Lord, thy God, thou shalt not have strange gods before Me.' And as well as that, of course, it used in reverse one of the most familiar of Catholic formats: confession. I'm sure many a client found the reversal mighty pleasant. Instead of laying bare your past life to a punitive priest, all one had to do was listen to motherly tones providing instruction in danger and desire. For just five bob. It had to seem worth it.

The sober-suited punters awaiting of the mistress of fate's cards, ball or tea-leaves were the most discreet and serious gamblers on the field. But there were plenty of opportunities for those with less metaphysical wagers to place. There were swarthy women in charge of wheel-'em-in stalls. You ran a coin down a groove onto a board of numbered squares; if your coin ended up in a square, not touching any of its borders, you won something – choice of stuffed toy, rubber ball or three glass marbles in a box. It was impossible, of course, but the first two or three pennies were a pleasure to throw away; one wheeled them in with a spendthrift's exuberance.

Then there was the three-card trick, all the more attractive for being illegal. The performer was as deft at shifting his little table (a cloth over a crate) as he was at switching the cards. The trick was made to look so easy, so enticing: any fool could do it. The cards moved with winning slowness, the queen virtually pausing for you to admire her sleek profile and sly, inward smile, so that you felt so absolutely, positively sure of her whereabouts that cupidity felt like a blessing. But just before you placed your hot little shilling on the sure thing some stranger in a black slouch hat would laconically throw down a quid, and collect handsomely. Well, maybe next time . . . . Then next time the trickster's hands flew among the cards with unprecedented finesse and stopped when least expected. Next time the befuddled bettor always lost.

It was strange the way that everything took its form from the occasion. Fortune-telling was gambling; the three-card trick was a compressed, exaggerated, hysterical version of racing. The stall-holders of the wheel-'em-ins and rifle range seemed the gentry's shady kin, reciprocal acts in the one circus, invisible save on this day of the sporting chance. We, the public, were the enticeable, naïve, unassertive world they dealt with.

And yes, it was impossible to ignore the gentry, finally. This was not just because the races were held on the Castle Farm, or because the voice that announced the runners and riders was posh and lofty. It wasn't even because race-day was the one day in the year that they revealed themselves as a community. I surreptitiously eyed them diving into hampers and swigging out of hip-flasks under the stand of beech by the road, well back from the common throng. They produced extraordinarily handy items, such as rugs to lounge on, field-glasses and shooting-sticks, which to me were the acme of class and common sense. They brayed and squawked to their hearts' content in their own lingo. They roared into view in shooting-brakes and Land-Rovers. Their women wore trousers. And of course they owned just about all the horses.

It wasn't even this last fact that impressed the gentry on me.

I was only interested in the horses inasmuch as they were the pretext for this saturnalia of jeopardy and cash. The racing itself was terrible. Mutinous animals being flogged over hedges and ditches: that's all it amounted to, as far as I could see. I much preferred the bookies, the syntax of their sign language, their outsized doctors' bags, their strange, energetic cries, 'Three-to-one, bar one! Five-to-one the field.'

I was too small to see much. And in any case the races took place mainly out in the country; most of the time all anyone could see were figures flitting beyond the branches of the naked trees. Still, it was possible to get a taste of the race if you stood by a jump. There one caught the sensational urgency of approaching hoofs and the moments of strained silence as, with a sound like fibre tearing, the snorting, airborne steeds had their bellies struck by the jump's mane of brushwood.

Standing by a jump had a couple of drawbacks, however. One was that it was impossible to get back to see the finish in time. The other was that every so often a horse fell and, as the official phrase went, had to be destroyed. The poor thing would strive to right itself, wild-eyed, frothing, whinnying with terror and pain. But all its efforts only made a shallow grave in the moist, spring earth. The vet went to his case. The slim, brass-barrelled humane-killer was applied to the temple. A last lurch and –.

Finishes frightened me too, though. Not the desperate striving of the hacks to be past the post and out of this; not the giant, bony figure of the great McLernan (champion jockey of all east Munster) stretched taut in the stirrups, welting his mount to glory; not the clash of rival tributes in the turbulent crowd. What frightened me, and forcefully reminded me that the gentry were no mere presence, but power, was the whipper-in. He too went on horseback and wore an official colour, though not the gay silks of jockeys, but the blood-red blazer of the huntsman (and, as I thought, the soldier). His job was to clear the way along the run-in to the winning-post, and he managed to press the crowd back quite simply: by riding as close to it as he possibly could and waving aloft, in threat, his riding-crop. 'Get back!' he barked. 'Make way!'

In his reckless policing and scarlet coat and horrid unenjoyment on his face, he seemed a hellish figure. He'd run you down as quick as he'd look at you. He's brute force, I thought, he doesn't give a damn; he's everything I heard about the English in the terrible days gone by. His presence suggested that I was quite wrong to think that race-day was all looseness, all squandering, all pleasure. He was purpose and order. He was alien, hostile. He charged at us with the force of a law, terrifying us for our own good.

I ran from him like a chastised whelp, and although, he was especially careful not to touch anyone and I realized, however inarticulately, that he was not a throw-back, not a symbol, not a force of destiny, but really only a jacket on a horse, my mind was turned into a tissue of painful smouldering, as though a branding-iron had touched it. I saw power without substance, force without salience, form without tact. For maybe twenty seconds I felt spurned and trodden down. Twenty seconds was plenty.

3

The whipper-in put the heart crossways on me, yet I felt free to repudiate him. His behaviour was hateful: I hated him right back. I don't think older people were quite able, or willing, to be so cut-and-dried in their reactions – and I mean not only in their reactions to the whipper-in, whose mode of discipline they seemed to approve, shouting commands of their own to support his, but also to the gentry at large. They seemed in some way tied psychologically to the gentry's presence.

The tie took various forms. For one thing, the valley had no history of rebelliousness: poaching was about the only form of local deviance – by no means a trivial one, to my mind, but one which has no place in the legends of the national struggle that were handed down to us (which may be unfortunate). And then when I saw those old lads admiring Royal Tan, or when I noticed Moss and his cronies doffing their caps as an elegant black roadster swished by, or even at the races looking at gaggles of elderly labourers leaning on the paddock fence and gazing in deep amaze at the steaming, exemplary creature 79 now being fussed by the foulard fraternity (I wonder where they got those neckerchiefs, the ones with the pattern of amoeba swimming on a piss-yellow field) – simply being present in the particular theatre of gestures suggested to me that some principle of unity, or at least of implication, was at work.

I even saw it at home. Staunch though Mam was in her nationalist affections – none stauncher: she'd bite the head off anyone who dared murmur a demurral – she still bought a Poppy every year. There weren't many in the town who were invited to, either. But Miss Anson always came to our house and received a half-crown to remember the fallen of Flanders by. And if Geo objected he was soon made to desist. Of course, Mam had her own memories of the Great War, of the boys she knew who never came back from it (quite a number volunteered to go from loyal Lismore). Her first daughter was born on Armistice Day; she was christened Mary but known forever as Peace. And what did Georgie know?

It must have been hard for his generation. The patterns of close attachment between master and man had loosened considerably by the time George came into his manhood, and responsibility for moral exemplification had passed entirely to the officers of another empire, the clergy. No wonder he, my father and my father's Dublin friends had no time for priests. Yet there were elements of the whipper-in about Geo too, in his fiery temper, his unpredictable vitality, his ability to make me fear him. But it was all unwitting. The instrument on horseback acted deliberately, secure in his power for the time being. George struck out blindly, innocently, as though through the bars of a cage, as though to snap for good his real and imagined bands.

My generation, perhaps, is the first to be in a position to disregard loyalty either to Christ or to Caesar. It is tempting to think so – since I'd like to be proud of my generation. Besides, it makes excellent cultural sense to take the gentry's invisibility at face value, and to regard priests as simply religious functionaries. But I'm not in sufficiently close contact with my generation to know if it thinks along these lines. Maybe it's tempting to hope for the best, for a set of liberating loyalties, because it seems to me now that such a possibility existed when I was growing up. Though, of course, I may be able to say that only because possibility exalts every childhood; it's the hallmark of the child's openness and ignorance.

The vestiges of loyalty that I observed around me were hard to understand. I took them to be reminders of continuity, but the continuum to which the village's star had been hitched was, as far as I could see, going nowhere. Yet, I suppose when centuries of continuity stall, the mechanisms which kept it running smoothly for so long are bound to run on a little, fuelled by compulsiveness and uncertainty. No generation should ever take upon itself the task of undoing the work of a few hundred predecessors, though in order to achieve anything at all it probably has to believe it can. In Lismore, however, there was nobody equal to the job, no heroic consciousness to facilitate a return to the days before the Duchy.

Just as well, no doubt; complexity is more nourishing to the spirit than reverie. There was no concept of complexity, either, though. There was a landscape – a mindless, enduring litter of evidence.

Even before King John was a twinkle in his daddy's eye, the valley had been settled by monks and monastery. And even before that there must have been something going on at the Round Hill, a mound two miles east of town overlooking the river, from which the town takes its name. God only knows what such a druidic remnant really represents.

We know that Edmund Spenser knew the valley. So did Sir Walter Ralegh, and an impoverished Robert Boyle, afterwards Earl of Cork, and who knows who else of their contemporaries besides. The valley was a natural attraction for coast-hugging, westward-tending adventurers – I assume they hugged the coast as long as they could, for protection. And the Blackwater estuary was the first major one they would have come to without a sizeable fortified town at its mouth.

There is a town there now, of course, Youghal, but I don't think it was there to any extent before Ralegh came in from the ocean and built a jail on the site. The town in those parts long ago was Ardmore, home of a celebrated round tower, a much more impressive and more mystical edifice than Lismore Castle. It's easier for me to appreciate the tower for what it is, rather than for what it represents. Of course, it can be made to stand for the solitary, embattled and enduring Church, beacon of the Dark Ages when only Irish monasticism stood between the Northmen and the lights going out all over Europe. But it's a strain to employ such terms; the struggle against darkness is no longer being waged on remote beach-heads in County Waterford. Unlike the Castle, the tower is historically complete: its meaning is bounded by the era of its service. And although still intact, in every other respect it's like all the other ruined abbeys and disused graveyards that dot the country from top to bottom – a placid, assimilated shell. An icon, the invisibility of whose inner life is entirely appropriate. But it wasn't on an estuary, and so Youghal was an ideal point of entry, wide, welcoming waterway. To express a thought too sacrilegious for nationalists, once again – in the wake of King John – nature was not on the side of the natives. The river was tidal. So, up came Gloriana's crew: nothing to stop them.

What did they see, those *conquistadores*, stealing up that still, accommodating river? Green slopes on either bank, rising gently, densely, as though they were the dark waters reproduced in an even more permanent form. Penumbrous, impenetrable. They met the river's unexpected, right-angle sweep west at Cappoquin, where there was nothing, nothing to attack or appropriate. Then, at last, Lismore, the Castle – the relief of seeing in that fastness something recognizably their own.

They sailed in clear and free. No people. If the forests harboured natives, they showed no sign. The land existed in a state of perfect integrity: aqueous, unmoving, arboreal, silent. A cathedral, a queen, a virgin. Like the James River, the Charles River, Potomac, Hudson – the penetrations without number later on. And it so little resembled property, being undefended. The urge to possess it, to seize it like a treasure, to treasure it so jealously that power became the sole metaphysic of occupancy . . . . That urge must have been as irresistible as an event in the subconscious. To pitch picturesquely, to shed blood, burn and starve in honour of possessions . . . . That lust to grasp this peace at all costs, this unmanned world, this kingdom without factions . . . . From what did such unstaunchable desire arise, this sacrilege-sized need to rupture the chaste greenery and husband it, this immense impulse to settle, as though the object of adventuring were anchorage, refuge, port after stormy sea?

And out of the husbandry grew a mind. The ardour of their lordships' eyes perceived the valley in a wholly new way. Their longing was secular, material. They freely thought the world their plaything; there was nobody to put a check on their avarice. The mind they fostered was called 'property'. Once mindfulness was installed, once a scale of values was introduced (whether consciously as an intellectual habit or just as a means of attempting to calibrate lust), once ownership became a synonym for living – then the beauty turned terrible. The place could never be just a place again. In addition, making immodest the whole accident of locality, there would be somebody's sense of it to cope with. The valley lost its nature and entered history. The appropriators, who retained the freedom of mind to do whatever they pleased, pretended that this didn't happen, or behaved as though history meant green reverie. Which was their undoing, requiring more freedom than they knew how to contain, eliminating challenge, corrupted by absolute power, their aftermath the mock-heroic present of my childhood with its stagnation, emigration and the new invaders, tourists.

Coming up from a swim in the strand we'd see them disembarking, strange number plates, sometimes from remote parts of Ireland, oftener from England: BMD, VEX and GB stuck on the rear, which we translated with somewhat wistful sarcasm as 'going back'. The party usually consisted of Mum and Dad and an aged parent – the wife's mother, I always thought, having formed the impression from BBC comedy shows that she couldn't be kept out of anything. The women smoothed their frocks and Dad filled his pipe and they crossed the road to gaze blankly at the inscrutable Castle.

What did they make of it, those Magellans of the Morris Minor? I suppose for most of them it was just another roadside attraction, one more historical float in the procession of Ireland's eye-catching vistas and edifices. A five-minute stop could hardly allow for much experience, nor could the couple of lines in the AA book that might have influenced them to take the road through Lismore. And as for the semi-willed fortuitousness of their possessing the resources to be in our midst in

83

the first place, the very fact that they lived with notions of mobility and choice, those were factors enabling them to view the Castle innocently, with wonder, as a prop in fairyland. Did they know how lucky they were to be savouring history without complexes, to gaze in restful amazement at what was so above and beyond them?

Who knows what they knew? Their gazetteers and handbooks gave them some information – quoting Thackeray on the Blackwater, 'the Irish Rhine', assuring them that the Castle was indeed a splendid example of something or other, but closed to the public. No information, apart from that regarding privacy, was available at the site. And the tourists never spoke: that is, sometimes they asked a question of the men sitting on the first arch, but they never even bothered to look at us. Usually instead of words, a camera was produced – one of the Castle, *snap*: one of the reach of river eastward to the hazy upland; one of the women, the Dad, to our envious approval, commemorating his presence by self-effacingly, though decisively, operating the machinery.

It didn't bother us in the slightest that we were ignored. That way we could observe at our ease Mum in her cotton-print and cardigan, bent-kneed Mother in tweed, spindly, shirt-sleeved Dad. In fact, it seemed appropriate now, picturing that endlessly repeated summer scene, that it largely consisted of a dumb-show, in which it wasn't clear who was looking at what and what exactly they were seeing – a pantomime of gesture and façade.

Besides we were too buoyant from our swim to feel anything one way or another about strangers. Where we swam, however, was not the Blackwater. What we called the Strand was the Abh' na Sead, a small tributary of the big black one which raced down the mountain, draining sheep-pastures. There was a pool there in which we splashed and floundered all summer long, and where later on (show-offs home from boarding-school) we learned to smoke and, much less rewardingly, hid in bushes on the girls' side. We could have swam in the Blackwater. Lads from Church Lane did, down at the rock. But it was only the likes of those reckless, unselfconscious ones that could give their all to fighting the terrible undertow. We weren't able: at least we were warned not to, as though our people knew that we hadn't the strength or heart for such disporting.

Tourists were not confined to family saloons, however, and in their other manifestation, the bus, we found them somewhat more of a tease. This was due to their arrival in force, partly: it really made us feel that the town was something and that the age of the horse-and-cart was surely doomed to see the bridge clogged with two or three tour-buses.

The buses themselves were a stimulus, being quite different from the common single-decker that made the thrice weekly run between Fermoy and Dungarvan. The tourers weren't even in green: they sported a greeny-yellow, rather insipid, livery, and the seats seemed to be raised up, and the high roof was in tinted glass.

The exotic aura of these roadsters was completed by the name of an Irish river festooned in scrollwork on the front, painted on a little more darkly than the livery, for all the world looking like weedroots under water, slant and entangled. How many of those names, to our chagrin, we never recognized at all! Funshion, Maigue, Fergus, Garavogue . . . . We recovered promptly from our embarrassing ignorance by telling our-selves that the strange names meant that Ireland was a real country, after all, containing unknowns of its own, vouchsafed to us by visiting Yanks.

In the normal course of events, Yanks were no big deal. Badger Crowley, for example, was a nice old guy, but he seemed just a little out of place – those nice lightweight check suits of his made him stand out, and his seersucker seemed a species of misjudgment. On the other hand, the old rip who lived out the country, Paddy the Gas, who spent every cent of his fat pension on drink for himself and his numerous buddies, seemed to be all the more a misfit from fitting in too well. It must have been that they just couldn't belong. When Billy Whelan from Massachusetts arrived one day in school we were told to call him 'Puncán' which we did with a will, exult-ing in the bastard freedom of prejudice.

But those three were returned Yanks, people who'd come home to stay. The tourists were real Yanks, just riding through. They fascinated us. We'd seen their movies, heard their songs, knew their twangy accents. Now we were getting to see them, live – inhabitants of the future we desired for

85

ourselves (money, cars, blondes), war-winners, bulwarks against the red menace and the yellow peril. And a lot of them were good Catholics.

And they looked so healthy, these Yanks, tall, tan, plump: the only blemish we could see was that they all seemed to wear spectacles. Their clothes were great: devastating checks, shirts like postcards of a tropical paradise, big-butted matrons in cerise dungarees. You could tell by their appearance that they didn't give a damn what anyone thought of them. That was the kind of freedom we craved – to be able to tell the world to bugger off, to turn ourselves into sartorial Caesar's salads precisely as and when it pleased us, to stare vacantly into the middle distance with cigars the size of small trees clamped between jaws smooth as steel. They're children at heart, we thought, wishing that we could think of ourselves as half so gay and simple.

Sometimes they spoke – even to us kids, but more often to the group of elders who pitched their long afternoons in the vicinity of the bridge, half-hoping for a word from a stranger. 'Say now . . . ' and some historical question would follow. The natives would point fingers in uncharacteristically animated response, while the visitors nodded. Then, his thirst for knowledge temporarily slaked, he might say, 'I guess you men would take a drink', hand rummaging in a capacious pocket, carillon of loose change, forelocks touched, air thick with the sound of 'Sir'.

It happened too that every so often a bus would have an American 'young wan' on board, travelling with her parents, of course, but really (we knew) a true daughter of destiny in her own right. Destiny was pretty loosely defined, but we knew what we meant, a combination of economic ease and titillating peccadilloes. Usually, we seldom gave a girl a second look; that didn't come until we were fourteen or fifteen, by which time we found the girls at pains to ignore us. But glimpsing a blonde faun through the windows of a tour bus inspired us to manic antics. We'd race the bus as it dragged up the New Way and install ourselves, panting, at the Red House corner to watch her daintily alight – her blue-jeans the very robe of romance! – to take tea in the Devonshire Arms Hotel.

She'd look at us, of course she would, we hotly debated,

waiting till she completed her toothsome morsel (we saw cool fingers ply the cutlery, pearly incisors tear daintily at the cooked ham sandwich). Didn't she hail from where O'Brien and Murphy were as sound a name as any? But she never did look; neither eyebrow raised nor eyelash flickered. Demurely up the steps she climbed. The bus sprang to life. Our necks jerked forward, taut with the tense desire to speak, numb in ignorance of what the right approach was. Would shouting 'Elvis Presley' offend? How about whistling something by Pat Boone, 'Love Letters in the Sand', say?

No good, no good. She'd already gone, leaving us with just a haze of blue exhaust smoke to wave at. It was time for our own tea. We turned from one another to go. 'See ya,' we said, 'See ya', in laconic series. It felt as though a form of unity had been dispelled, as though we'd thought we were going somewhere, only to realize that indeed we were not.

IV

THE OTHER EMPIRE

1

'Confiteor Dei . . . ,' said Peter Hickey, and paused uncertainly.

'Go on, Seoirseen,' said Brother Murphy with snide impatience.

'Om-ni-po-ten-ti,' I managed.

'*Omnipotenti*,' the master repeated and, grabbing my pal Pete's arm, banged the point of his elbow sharp against the edge of the desk. We were going to be altar boys. One of the curates had come to school to talk it over with Brother Murphy, and a selection was made, mainly of lads like me and Pete, scions of Main Street, with a few make-weights from Botany and the country thrown in for the sake of appearances (Church Lane didn't make the grade).

Chrissy and Mam were overjoyed. So they had been when I graduated from the convent infant school and went to primary proper at the Brothers. And when I made my First Communion it was a miracle. They seemed to think there was something unlikely and very special about my arrival at such junctures, and regarded my having made it thus far with fond relief, my conforming to the common path a source of great reassurance to them.

An additional delight for Mam was that for each of these arrivals I had to dress the part, so she was able to express the seamstress in herself. Making something for me enabled her to see me simply as a child. Otherwise, she regarded me as a child-concept, the concept being that I was a responsibility which she was discharging not just on my father's behalf but on nature's. She was proud to discharge it, and needless to say I was very glad to have her – without her I believed I would be lost. But her awareness of her role was a constant reminder that I wasn't hers, a reminder reinforced by her seldom having time to play, her infrequent gestures of physical closeness, her never giving presents.

With Chrissy and George I felt I was theirs because they were so often ready to sing, to play, to draw me out. I still feel more theirs than anybodys, despite all the water that's between us, all the ink – despite, above all, my unconquerable urge to redeem and comprehend our deep life together in that small no-place.

Mam, though, was a lot warmer to me than to her own. She was forever harassing and reproving them. Their autonomy frustrated her. She criticized their behaviour as though its sole aim and object was to make her account to herself for it. Every so often there were complete breaks, during which the name of a certain aunt could not be mentioned. Some of these breaks lasted years.

But perhaps Mam could only see her world as a round of duty and responsibility. Her view expressed the onus of being flawless, unflinching, singular, which her generation assumed, for only in rigorous adherence to a militant faith could the victory of the people be assured and the soul of fecklessness, induced by the foreigner's psychic sway, be remade.

Dress-making, however, had nothing to do with this. It belonged to the days of her girlhood – an unmarried, unbloodied zone, before the Great War, before Tans burst in on sleep and made her children howl. So she took to fitting me for the altar with quiet, deep-seated glee.

The scarlet material for the soutane and the linen for the surplice were sent specially from Dublin. Peggy dashed into town to Clery's during her lunch-hour for them. (Peggy is another aunt; she lives with my father, cooks him dinner and plies the Hoover at weekends, reminds him in all innocence of what's missing. They don't get on too well.) And of course it was impossible to find a suitable length of lace to trim the surplice with anywhere else except the capital, so poor Peg had to spend two or three Saturdays trying to find what was right. Most boys' surplices had borders of stuff that looked like the first cousin to net-curtaining. That wouldn't do us, though. If God tolerated such inadequacy that was His business. O'Briens required more.

92   Meanwhile, Brother Murphy was rehearsing the Latin with

us – pinching and punching and pulling our hair to his heart's content – and acquainting us with the parts of the mass. It conferred an impressive sense of maturity to be on speaking terms with the priest's arcana. Collect, Epistle, Secret, Agnus Dei . . . I felt starry-eyed with insiderdom. And then there was the privileged tongue itself.

To some extent, of course, all of us at school were bi-lingual, thanks to compulsory Irish. But everyone thought Irish was useless. It didn't tell us anything we didn't know. The textbooks dealt with sheep, fields, hills and children. A world was depicted which we knew infinitely better through the medium of our first language, English, and from the everyday evidence of our own eyes. For reasons best known to our educational lords and masters the rattling old far-fetched stuff of the sagas was kept from us. So instead of the stampeding action of *An Táin*, imaginative nourishment came in the Palladium's diet of westerns, with Gabby Hayes and Walter Brennan on hand to make us proud of being Irish, in the unlikely event of anyone remembering, while partaking of the sagebrush, that he had a nationalist, or any other kind of, consciousness.

But Latin was different. Nobody spoke it, yet it underwrote a world which was much more coherent and imposing (a world of rank, of remote controls, of refulgent embodiments, of a ruler who held sway from beyond the sea) than anything the Gael possessed. There was no need to speak it, to apply it demotically. The repetition of sanctified, pre-ordained formulae accomplished more than common language could dream of. Its inutility was unquestioned, as though only through its uselessness could it uphold mystery and portend beauty. And there were its sounds. Even if the words themselves stuck like glue in our mouths, how could we resist their sonorities: 'Orate fratres', 'Sursum corda', 'Ad deam qui laetificat juventutem meam'?

And then, at last, the big day, my first serving. Neophytes were supposed only to make the responses and just watch while their more experienced colleagues served by deed. But in my case that didn't happen. Jim Linneen overslept, so Edmund Nugent and I had to go it alone. This was exactly what I wanted, of course, centre-stage from the start, and Edmund steered me kindly, giving me the water, which   93 according to rote would have meant my having the book as well, only I didn't, it being too heavy – and if I let it fall . . . !

It was lovely being so near the priest, the credence-table, the gem-studded chalice, the surreptitious colloquy ('Suscipe, Domine . . . ': 'Hic est enim corpus . . . '), the snap of the host being split for the priest's communion. Mam and Chrissy were loud in their praises and gave me an extra slice of fried bread for breakfast. By the end of the week – the serving stint began with first mass (8 a.m.) Sunday morning, followed by mass every morning at the same time and ending with second mass (11) the following Sunday – I had it all off pat.

Being an altar boy was the first experience I had of completeness. I was aware that it was possible, naturally; I knew that being in a state of grace promised it, and of course I had approached the communion rail with all my sins washed away, all my flaws annulled, and in a fit state to receive the body of Christ into my heart and into my mind. But all that, soothing though it could be, was insubstantial, temporary, abstract. It didn't lay its material under my hand. It wasn't complicated. It offered nothing to be mastered, no movement, no timing, no lifting, no utterance. Above all, no novelty. Sublime surrender as a member of the congregation was all very well, but it couldn't compare to the neophyte's élite officiating. The notion that the show couldn't go on without me gave rise to a feeling of integration as pleasurable as when, far less often, I got all my sums right.

As with fractions or decimals, however, once I knew the method I knew everything, and serving grew to resemble everything else, rote and reflex alone sufficing. The novelty palled. But not the taste for novelty, though, which had the effect of making us squabble for leading roles.

'You had the patten yesterday, boy!'

'I want the bell, Butch.'

'The book – you can have the book.'

'Shove it. I want the wine.'

'Who's on the water?'

The best to have was the patten. We had two kinds. The old one, shaped like a sauce-boat, was dull, straw-colour. The new one was as round and resplendently golden as the pendulum of a king's clock.

94   What was best about being 'on' the patten, however, was

that you saw people as they never saw themselves. Holding it under the chins of the faithful as the priest dipped into the ciborium and laid a host on their tongues was great fun. The poses people struck! Some held heads forward humbly, like turtles; others threw back shoulders as though manfully to receive a punch; faces turned into plates or canisters or footballs or chimney-pots or letter-boxes. And tongues came in every shape and size. They were round, ridged, thin, narrow, flat, pitted, cracked, tumescent and never, never smooth. They were brick, cerise, vermilion, ox-blood, speck-led, lathered, slithery, cindery, sponge. Sour Mr Burke had a pale, pointy one. Mrs O., the gossip's, was large and lolloping. When you came across a particularly fine specimen you could give its owner a sly look on the street afterwards and confuse him.

Fun though that was, nothing could beat the solemn pleasures, and I mean pleasure: a feeling of radiance and of being stirred, not just of being tickled. This feeling came from the quasi-sacramental condition in which everything connected with the church reposed. Everything was blessed – the candles, the pews, the table in the sacristy on which Tom Heelan the sacristan, totalled up Sunday's collection, maybe even the canvas bags in which he lugged the take to the National Bank. But a blessing was invisible, just as 'the sacrifice' in 'the sacrifice of the mass' was. And just as the sacrifice was carried out by the priest on the faithful's behalf, making him at one with and distinct from his flock, so a blessing was a statement about the quality of objects used in the priest's business which relieved them of their merely physical character, made them tributaries of glory, artefacts of divine purpose, remotenesses.

Moving in such an environment induced a good deal of headiness, leading me, for one, to think the priest's appurte-nances more numinous, more enthralling, than the occasions of their use. Alb and cincture caught my fancy more readily than 'Dominuş Vobiscum'. The colour, needlework and cut of chasuble and maniple impressed me more than the reception of the communion wafer by my stainless soul. Sacristy outweighed sanctuary; sacristan was as intriguing as celeb-rant. Tom bearing monstrance, ciborium or chalice from the safe to the robing-table, right hand clad in a special white 95 glove, was as worthy as any priest.

Nothing would have been easier for me, I see, than to have become an out-and-out fetishist. But benediction saved me. Benediction had everything. And its diversions took place at exactly the right time, too, at the conclusion of tedious, inactive, repetitive Rosary. It was so good that those on the thurible or the candles for the altar didn't have to endure the whole Rosary but could go to light up around the fourth decade.

Both these jobs had certain drawbacks, however. One was that you were left out of the best bit of Rosary, the litany, the thrilling blazon – 'House of Gold', 'Tower of Ivory', 'Star of the Sea', 'Refuge of Sinners', and every type of Queen, Mother and Virgin besides. The dull voice of the congregation going 'Pray for us', 'Pray for us' couldn't dim the daring of those phrases.

Then, too, it was possible to get stuck with recalcitrant fire. Lighting the candles could be hell. Tom Heelan, possibly to torment us or (which is more likely) because it didn't occur to him, never set the candlewicks upright, so now and then it would be virtually impossible to apply the taper effectively. The wicks were too far above us to adjust manually, and for all we knew it might be a sin to do so, in front of the priest and everyone. So you just had to stand there, mortified, fuming, even praying for the cursed thing to ignite, arms aching from indecorously poking and craning at that measly, half-visible speck of black.

There was something to Mam's refrain: 'A wonder, now, the Canon wouldn't have a word with Tom about that.' But not one of us would hear a word said against Tom. That was mainly because he was so tolerant. He let us tie our soutanes around our necks by the top button, cloak-like, and horse around the headstones of the chapel yard – Batmen, Supermen, Phantoms. He told us stories about the Great War, in which he served. He even didn't mind Chainbreaker snapping off rivulets of candle-grease and chewing it, maintaining staunchly that there was nothing like it for curing warts (poor Chain had warts like the rest of us had dandruff).

Tom's war stories were remarkable. Here's a typical one.

'We were up there by the Siegried line,' said Tom, pointing his pipe towards the hurling field, 'and I was showing the top brass around, Churchill and them. They were over to see our defences, y'see, and the officer commanding was after asking me to do the honours. "Certainly, sir," says I, "anything to oblige." "Thanks awf'ly, Heelan," says he. Well there we were, the brains of the war, you might say, out beyond in no man's land, and I showed them this and that, answered their questions and all to that, when I let a bawl of "Duck, gentlemen!" out of me, like a shot out of a gun. Needless to say, they all thrun themselves on the ground and not a peep out of them. Five seconds later, not fifty feet away, up goes a grenade. Well, yer men got to their feet, brushed themselves down and, of course, were all over me. I could have had any medal I wanted. "But how on earth did you manage to do it?" says they. "A thing of nothing," says I, cool as a breeze. "I just happened to hear the Hun pull the pin."'

Evening after evening Tom regaled us with yarns like that, sitting on the stoop outside the sacristy, puffing judiciously on his acrid pipeful of Clark's Perfect Plug, a steady supply of which was the height of his ambition, a figure beyond the range of candles and devotions, a votary of quite a different sect, in fact, as he often gave us to believe, the British Army – let the gates of hell (Russia) try to prevail against it!

Another thing Tom never gave a hand with was lighting the thurible. If anything, this was a worse chore than the candles. Charcoal was used as thurible-fuel, and to get a piece going the flame of a match was held to its edge until some heat was retained (usually several matches later), at which point it was blown to a glow. Establishing the approved condition could be a nerve-wracking experience, and often, in desperation, pieces of taper were broken off and used as a base, with whole tablets of charcoal thrown on top of it. The result was a conflagration, the climax of which came when the priest sprinkled the incense on and, in a crackling gush, a billow of divine scent arose, the whole effect an imitation of what popping heavenly corn must be like.

My favourite thing to be on at benediction was the incense boat, but really anything would do. It was a struggle to detach the full-length, cloth-of-gold cope from its cruciform, cherrywood stand, and lift it onto the priest's shoulders, but I felt strong and manly from the struggle – proud, too: the stand was a piece of my grandfather's craftsmanship. Then there was the humeral veil, which had to be collected from the   97 credence table just before the priest raised the monstrance and which slithered richly round his shoulders. It too was cloth of gold, and on the back it bore a device, a lamb fashioned from little pearls, curled up in the shelter of a semi-circular sunburst. At the heart of the sun were the mysterious initials IHS. We fought over what they meant. 'I have suffered.' ''Tis not, boy. I have sinned!'

Even the bell was better at benediction, because the priest faced out, bearing aloft the magnificent monstrance, the spokes of gold surrounding its window suggestive of a sun which beamed down fair weather forever. And it was fun to time the three trills of the bell to occur between the three times the thurifer went *chock-chock-chock* as he rattled the pot on the chains, honouring the host with his home's supreme aroma.

In fact, it was possible to be on nothing at all and still get a great kick out of benediction. The smell, the light, the smoke, the glitter: these were intoxicants, thought-purgers, sweet-meats for the senses. Something as plain as standing for the final hymn had a deliciousness to it – Moll striving with the squally organ, the ragged voices of the congregation, the strange sensation of engenderment that the gold and smoke conveyed, Father Murphy's nasal tenor as he swayed back and forth, keeping time, everyone together: 'Oh Mother! / Tell me / What am I to do?'

Sometimes money changed hands. Priests home on holiday from America or the African missions tipped a shilling – enough for two glasses of ice-cream at Hogan's, three visits to the gods at the Palladium for the Sunday matinée, or one sixty-four page comic. Not bad. We felt we earned it for having been kept an extra half-hour from breakfast.

And there were weddings, which paid a little more, but which were rather more rare than visiting priests. A lot of people just didn't get married. Besides, England had claimed the majority of the town's eligible partners.

When somebody from Lismore did marry, the ceremony almost invariably took place outside the parish, sometimes because that was where the intended came from, often because the thought of having all the neighbours watching was unbearable. It was a great thrill for me to serve at the marriage of Billy Hogan and Kathleen Crowley, two people I knew well and was fond of. They made a smashing couple, I thought, all smiles (and I got a good tip). Usually, though, the couples were strangers, red-faced country fellows in blue suits, girls in bottle-green frocks with, as the papers used to say, matching accessories. I don't remember many of the strange brides being in white, and a non-white wedding traditionally means something tainted, so I suppose that's why they travelled with their small retinues to our church: to keep their secret intact.

It always surprised me that even after the ceremony, the nuptial mass and papal blessing ('all the trimmings', as people said, as they might of a meal), the principals of the party were still nervous. They didn't seem to know if they were coming or going when they adjourned to the sacristy to sign the parish register. I had plenty of opportunity to observe them, removing my surplice and soutane as slowly and deliberately as possible in order to give the tip as much time as it needed to materialize. It was while studiously folding my robes that the best-man at last made his sheepish approach, tugged at my sleeve, whispering, 'Now, boy', to which the correct response was 'Ah, no', while, quick as lightning, pocketing the half-crown.

In all, though, weddings struck me as basically fugitive affairs. Funerals, on the other hand . . . . Well, they were not exactly galas, like a hurling match or the Cappoquin Regatta. But from all I heard at home I knew it was much more important to have a good funeral than a fine wedding. A good funeral was a demonstration of esteem, prestige and charity, and in a way they were much more enjoyable or, more accurately, much more characteristic of the life of the town and the values – not to mention the rhythm – which dictated its course. And for us servers they were enjoyable because they were our only real opportunity for genuine public appearances.

At funerals, however, our special status was plain for all to see. We walked on either side of the priest, between the crowd and the coffin. One of us carried the cross and another the bucket of holy water and sprinkler, the latter with what I thought was the best name in the whole liturgy, the aspergillum. Not more than two servers, normally. We knew that burial wasn't a sacrament, really, but felt that it really was kind-of. It was accompanied by, or gave rise to, the combina-

THE VILLAGE OF LONGING

tion of being at the same time pleasured and moved which, as far as I was concerned, was at the heart of holiness.

It wasn't the prayers that impressed me, though the 'De Profundis' had some rattling good lines – 'Et ipse redemit Israel ex omnibus iniquitatibus eis' fell from our mouths like a shovel of gravel. It wasn't even so much that the mechanics of burial intrigued me, although I was always relieved that interment went smoothly when Georgie had the arrangements, because he looked so flushed and uncomfortable in his suit. How things managed to go smoothly was, typically enough, beyond me: physical accomplishment and I were only rarely on speaking terms, and the interplay of boards and ropes as the coffin was being lowered seemed entirely a matter of touch and go, adding to the tension of relinquishing which gripped those standing impotently by.

What I liked was the unity. The six strong men, members of, or close to, the deceased's family, who stepped out of the crowd at the chapel and shouldered the coffin, arms intricately locked as they carried it slowly forth. The other men who came to take their place on the way to the graveyard, quietly insinuating their desire to honour. And behind us the silent crowd, the only sound the slur of footwear.

The dulled voice of subdued people praying. The hands of the bereaved being solemnly wrung again and again, and the layman's courtesy repeated and repeated: 'I'm sorry for your trouble . . . . ' Everyone was so genuinely present, so unreservedly committed to what was taking place.

'Et lux perpetua luciat eis', we responded, conscious of our own indifferent light, to be sure, but for once consoled by it, feeling that the deceased had the worst of it, and that we weren't too badly off at all the way we were.

2

Were we religious at home?

100   We should have been. Lismore was one of the original Holy

Places, a fact still commemorated by our diocese being known as Waterford and Lismore. When the world was a know-nothing place, Lismore was endowed with learning. A thousand years or so ago it had a flourishing monastery. Proud kings' sons from lands beyond the sea sat on the bank of the river spelling out their lessons, their purple tunics fluttering in the mild morning breeze, while from the round tower one of the servants kept an eye out for those curse-o'-God Northmen – so well he might; the river was tidal as far up as Cappoquin, a mere four miles away. But the picture of the noble youths studying was a powerful lure used to persuade me, during my fairly frequent bouts of hypochondria, to stop whining and go on to school like everyone else. I didn't know, then, naturally, that the images of holiness, serenity and composure associated with monastic Lismore were nineteenth-century hand-me-downs. Still, it's amusing to think that perhaps Alfred the Great studied there as a stripling, and that he failed cookery.

The man – how dare I say 'Man!' He was a saint, of course – who ran the settlement (which everybody refers to as a university) is commemorated in the Irish name of the town: Lios Mór Mochuda. For reasons entirely beyond me Mochuda has been translated into English as Carthage, so Lismore has a Protestant and a Catholic church bearing his name, and a parish hall, and a number of citizens, including myself. My name is Seoirse Carthage. Mouthful as it is, and much as I detest it, I was spared the option of using it, unlike some others who had to sport it as a forename, local usage abbreviating it to Ca.

The reason I hate Carthage is that it sounds totally phony. 'Oh, but I *like* it,' insist well-meaning idiots to whom, in moments of weakness, I've confided it; 'It's cute.' It is not cute and I don't want them to like it. I don't want to bear a name whose first association for most people is not that it's the original of a great Irish family name (McCarthy) but synonymous with classical ruination. I don't want to have to explain my names.

It's a real shame that Carthage didn't perform a few miracles and get himself known beyond west Waterford. Not only would he have eased the way for his namesakes, not just in the matter of moniker, but career-wise. The tourism potential of a miracle-working Irish saint would be tremendous, particularly as, in a body, the Irish elect aren't worth a damn as miracle-workers. If they'd spent less time buried in books we'd all have soft jobs now. I'd be a guide conducting the halt and the lame through the hallowed precincts, pointing out the well (every saint has to have a well), the place where the crozier was found (a treasure of the Golden Age, on view at the National Museum), and so on (I'd be sure to think of other things), and the gateway to the Castle (which for the last eight hundred years has stood on the site of the monastery) would be hung with the crutches of Christendom.

As things were, it was not our lot to make a fortune flogging relics to gullible foreigners. It was not our lot to do anything at all about St Carthage. He was just – well, there, like every other historical thing: a thread in the tapestry, neither exploited nor effaced, simply admitted. I remember once a priest of ours decided to do something to mark the saint's feast, which occurs some time in the first half of May. The well was located and bunting hung and a little pilgrimage took place. The exercise lacked conviction, however, partly, I think, because there was some dispute over the site of the well. That derelict hole in the ground at the foot of Dowd's garden was a definite anticlimax to the pilgrimage. A much more plausible siting would be the source of the water that poured for local use through a wall of the Castle grounds and known as The Spout. But since access to the Castle was prohibited, and it was beneath our dignity to request entry, the hole had to do. Besides, as I'm sure the adults realized, a procession to the spout was impossible in view of the amenity's phallic overtones.

The net result of the abortive *feria* was the recognition that St Carthage did not impinge significantly on the spiritual life of the town. But what did?

For Georgie the answer to that question was simple: nothing. He didn't want a spiritual life. He was confident he could tell the difference between right and wrong. A just reward for the work of his hands was all he aspired to. So he was anti-clerical and irreligious largely on the grounds of personal irrelevance. Nevertheless, he never missed Sunday mass, though he took care to stand just inside the door unaccoutred by beads or prayerbook and with cronies (other devout mothers' sons) to converse with when something

102

sprang to mind. Having, apparently, no alternative but to go, it was necessary to treat being there inconsequentially. This attitude was sufficiently prevalent to be denounced from the pulpit every so often, not that that made a difference.

Professional animus fuelled Georgie's anti-clericalism too. The clergy never gave him work. Not that Georgie would have become a daily communicant if the parish priest contracted for him. But he did believe himself the best man for quality work, and justice as well as common sense surely dictated that the criterion of excellence, nothing else, made him worthy of his hire. After all, blast it, he was good enough to be hired by the toffs of the county, by Dean Stanley for work on the Protestant church, by Alec Ellis to attend to the Presbyterian church – but they were people who knew quality when they saw it, not like *pus mucha* Mike McGrath, who was still leaning over the half-door of the *bothán* he was born in . . . . Geo could rant an hour steady when he got going, the injustice of it all operating on him like a second mother.

The last straw for Geo was when the Canon decided to decorate the church. This was an unseemly decision in a general way, as Canon Walshe, his predecessor, was hardly cold in his grave before the new broom was produced. On top of that, a team of decorators was brought in from Cork, another county and another diocese, when it was giving work to the town he should be, not taking it away. And of course (it seemed fated), they didn't do much of a job, though admittedly they'd have their work cut out to please Georgie. The worst thing they did, in my view, was to efface most of the semicircular gallery of saints painted on the wall of the apse (the area behind the altar), leaving only St Patrick and St Carthage. None of the figures were named, but you could tell the national saint by the snakes, and if our own man wasn't left to us who else had a right to be? I don't know who exactly was painted out, but in all, four were. Surely St Declan of Ardmore was there, and St Colman of Fermoy, though his bailiwick was in the diocese of Cloyne. As for the other two I can only guess: St Otteran of Waterford City, St Finbarr of Cork? They were all fine, able-bodied men, anyhow, with lantern jaws and flowing, curly beards. Each was dressed in a full-length frock, grass green, ruby, violet or turquoise in colour. They had beady eyes. Hard men. Stern. They made a solemn distraction when mass dragged.

The work was as shoddy as the hiring principle, in Georgie's eyes. He must have remembered with some bitterness how freely his father had been called upon by canons and archdeacons of days gone by, and how his uncle Paddy, the smith, had fashioned the wrought-iron railings that separated the aisles. To be overlooked in favour of outsiders (and company men at that, not self-employed) must have felt like the confirmation of limbo.

Needless to say, had Georgie been contracted the glory reflected would have pleased me greatly. But the fact that he was virtually tradesmen-in-residence at the Protestant church was good compensation. I got to see things that none of the other lads did, except, of course, Tony Dowd and Har Allison, whose church it was. What going there in the devotional sense amounted to was impossible to say, attending alien service was a sin which only a bishop could expunge. But even empty and idle, the Protestant church was an intriguing place.

It was really ancient, much older than our church, indeed it had been our church until (so I was told) that sonovagun Cromwell stabled his horses in it – though, talk about an ill wind, that must have been when Mam's ancestor deserted, the man she had to thank for her posh maiden name, Willoughby (Georgie put it all together during wet days spent delving in the vestry). Inside, it wasn't a bit like ours. Not a lick of paint in the whole place, just walls of undressed stone which wept, scenting the air with clay. Not a holy picture, not a blessed statue, not a candle, not a station of the cross. If they were holy, they kept mighty quiet about it.

The best thing was the number of graves. They believed in burying indoors and out. Under shiny-smooth flagstones in the nave, soldiers and titled men reposed, indifferent to the world walking on them, which I found odd and eerie, especially when I was on my own. And there was a large area by the door to the belfry in which some vaults stood, containing the remains of bishops, I think; their ornate bulk deserved high-ranking tenants. These vaults unnerved me even more than the graves underfoot, partly because I wasn't used to thinking of the dead in terms of such edifices, and also because the stone they were built of contained traces of iron which had oxidized in the moist air, so that it seemed that the past was commemorating itself in its true, bloody, colour.

Dashing stealthily round the headstones in the yew-filled cemetery, wandering alone and small in the lofty, hollow interior, inspecting the skulls that Georgie's gravediggers brought up (orifices engorged with moist, yellow earth) – such interludes produced starts and shudders which undoubtedly had their delicious side (I was getting away with something). But, overall, the place oppressed me. Our church was richer, more colourful, more up-to-date. And, when I thought about it, that was only right. After all, weren't we, the Catholics, the bosses now? Let the Protestants be history if they liked: we were the present, and that was what I wanted. The melancholy Gothic of the lapsed overlord couldn't hold a candle to the brash red-brick of the people's choice. The very idea that it might be was, quite simply, unthinkable.

Much as Geo enjoyed working for Protestants – they let you get on with the job and paid promptly – he had no sense whatsoever of actually associating with them, any more than he felt that listening to the BBC day-in, day-out, might make him less of a nationalist. This strikes me now as another Irish cultural irony, Georgie's energetic, pragmatic style containing some of the cardinal qualities of the 'hard-riding country gentlemen' – quickness of eye, strength of hand, sureness of touch, vehemence of character. But, for all his excoriation of the ways of priestcraft, George acknowledged every year that he was born and bred a Catholic – that was all there was to it.

The acknowledgment was accentuated, though he wished it to be disguised, by its taking place just once annually, and not in Lismore. What happened was that every year around Easter, Geo and a carload of like-minded black sheep drove up into the Knockmealdowns to Mellary, Mount Mellary, the Cistercian monastery. There they'd 'scour the pot', make a clean breast of the year's excesses, such as they were – drink, temper tantrums, a fight or two, and if it was a good year a few quarter-hours of sex. To these he confessed, for them expressed himself truly sorry. He bent the knee, assuming – with, for once, no disagreement – the passivity of his people.

I never went to Mellary with George – the car always left too early in the morning – but I was there tons of times with Chrissy. Thursday was half-day in Lismore, so the girls who 105 served behind the counters of their brothers' shops were free. What better, then, than to don the rouge and powder, the navy-blue costume, and hire a car to go to confession. Chrissy and Mam joined in, I was squeezed between a couple of ample, happy penitents, and off we'd putter in Dinny Reagan's A40. These excursions took place quite regularly: they were a species of dating.

The Cistercians struck me as a strange lot. They got up at half-two in the morning to sing their office, they weren't allowed to speak (though they could smile), and they dug a bit of their graves, or so I was told, every day. Other orders came down to us, and preached. But we had to drive up to the men who, as a rule, kept mum. Naturally, confession proceeded as usual, and they did have a man in the bead shop selling holy trinkets, who talked enough for the whole community, bright chatter, a bird in a stone cage. And I suppose the man running the guest-house spoke – the guest-house was a strongly recommended retreat for people trying to kick the bottle. I'm sure it was very refreshing for adults to deal with clergy whose first concerns were neither prurient nor related to parochial funds. But I could never accept that anyone would volunteer for such a limited life, with only the blue, indifferent mountains for company.

The wedding principle of going away from home to feel at ease seemed to serve confessing, too. Maybe the thought of confiding in, of being vulnerable before, a perfect stranger was enticing. Not that it was felt that the confidentiality of the confessional at home would be violated. Just probably that peace of mind came more readily knowing you wouldn't meet the figure on the far side of the grille out walking his dog or at the Whist Drive. But what did these confessors know of the world of sin? And did ignorance make them severe, doling out sibilant chastisement and lengthy penances? Perhaps it was accepted that monks, being holier (being less in the toils of history and family, that is), would be wrathful. Besides, the more vividly the penitent felt the lash, the sweeter the accompanying salve seemed.

Or maybe the monks' greater proximity to God enabled them to see frailty through the eye of eternity, making them lenient. At any rate the women loved them. The mountains' cold shoulders, the narrow rule, the unknowable confidante –

106

did they subliminally identify with renunciation and its unspoken similarity to something in their own lives, and, were they thus temporarily appeased? I only know that everyone was happy going home: the car was full of 'Oh, a lovely man . . . a saintly man', and smug cigarette smoke.

Despite these trips, which she took quite as seriously as any of her companions, Chrissy stays in my mind as a sinner. I should hasten to add that Mellary afternoons were by no means the only indications of her commitment. Like most women of the town, and to a greater degree than a lot of them, Chrissy was involved in the Church's elaborate network of subsidiary devotional obligations, participation in which, as we were frequently reminded from the pulpit, was the true mark of a *real* Catholic.

Chris was a member of the women's branch of the Sacred Heart Confraternity and saw to it that the members of her guild were fully paid-up. (In everything connected with the Church, the hand in the pocket and the open purse were the inevitable accompaniment to the bent knee and the sign of the cross.) And Chrissy was a Child of Mary, meaning, as far as I could see, that she belonged to a secret society. The Children of Mary held their meetings in the convent, and appeared in public in blue cloaks and long white veils, singing. I suppose it was some sort of virginity action group.

Then there was the choir, if that's what the ailing organ and the handful of disheartened vocalists could be called. Nobody gave a damn about the choir, not even to the extent of declaring that we'd all be better off if it shut up. Chrissy's relationship with it was erratic. Sometimes when Kate, the regular organist, couldn't play, Chris would take charge. But it was too much for her, and it must have been thought impolite to practise, since she never bothered. Mainly she sang: 'Panis Angelicus' during the offertory at second mass, 'Ave Maria' (Gounod) on the Feast of the Immaculate Conception. A thin voice, but true, and so superior to anything else available that it seemed excessive, out of place.

Yet months could pass without her going near the choir. I preferred it that way. Her solos embarrassed me. One reason they did was my sense of Mam's lack of enthusiasm for them, which to me was tantamount to adverse judgment. Also, I believed that there was something obscurely sinful in being out on one's own in church, in exhibiting an extravagance of self, in sending shivers distractingly down the spines of the faithful (well, they went down mine and I didn't know what to do). It was much better when Chrissy came with Mam and me into the body of the congregation and I could observe her busy with her beads, head slightly tilted to the right, a preoccupied and semi-afflicted expression on her fine-boned face. No music. All self submerged in a welter of private prayer.

It wasn't because of the choir that I have my picture of Chris the sinner, even though I had been solemnly warned off the organ loft because it was an occasion of sin (people who were too respectable to stand inside the door with Georgie went up there for a chat), and even though I'd had experience of Chrissy's music sinning against me. But there was one thing that did influence my conception of her fallen condition: Lough Derg. St Patrick's Purgatory, a bleak island in the black north, was known as a place of pilgrimage since at least the time of Calderón de la Barca. Surely, I said to myself (a desire for justification my only perspective), nobody would go there unless he was made to.

The journey up was punishment enough for anyone, the way Chrissy told it. First, there was the trial by land, the bus. For people unused to venturing beyond their own parish, two hundred miles of twisty roads by bus was a right stomach-turner, especially since all aboard were smoking like chimneys, trying to get enough nicotine put by to survive the three smoke-starved days ahead. Then there was trial by water, taking the boat over to the island fastness. And finally the place itself, unalterably devoted to retaining the stars it had earned in medieval Michelins: dry bread, black tea, water.

It may have been just as well to arrive as sick as a dog, like Chris's group. That way the place's revenge on the flesh might not have seemed so drastic, having been unwittingly anticipated. It may have been too, though, that no matter what condition you arrived in you couldn't really be prepared. The regimen punished everyone. Either the fasting did for them, or they couldn't stand the all-night prayer sessions, or they baulked on finding their feet in flitters from having to circle the stony surround of St Patrick's Basilica barefoot.

108   Only someone like Mam's friend Annie could relish that

sort of thing. She was what I called holy, much holier than Mam, even. They'd been friends since girlhood, their friendship surviving the years Annie spent in New York looking after rich children. 'You'd think she wasn't a day away,' said Mam proudly: Lismore *über alles*. Now Annie lived in Botany and had nothing but faded cotton frocks, a long, sensual, melancholy face, and a faith that lived like a flame.

She knelt in the front seat, gospel side of the centre aisle, underneath the pulpit, her head thrust forward with a leftward list, looking for all the world like St Teresa of Avila, St Catherine of Sienna, St Monica, Our Lady of Dolours . . . . At any rate, not like a local. Not like an Irishwoman. And certainly not like an Irish woman saint, because apart from the formidable Brigid and Dymphna, patroness of the insane, there aren't any – odd, in view of all the powerful women to be found in the sagas, Maeve, Deirdre, Grainne . . . .

Anyhow, there she'd be, morning and evening, hail, rain or snow, suffering and supplication written all over her face. When responses were called for – at Rosary, for example – she called out hers loud and long, savouring the throbbing tones every syllable: 'As / it / was / in / the / be / gin / ning / is / now / and / ever / shall / be; lead / us / not / in / to / temp / ta / tion; now / and / at / the / hour / of / our / death / A / men.' And during benediction she'd sing, an opulent, off-key contralto, dolefully belling:

> To-o Je-sus' heart all bu-hur-ning
> With fer-vent lo-hove fo-hor men.

That was it, for me, the real thing. Annie looked just like the pictures of those holy women, all stigmatized by the ache of their ardour. She had sailed the Atlantic, beheld the lights of Broadway, soothed infant heirs of Amagansett, and still she craved and cried out. And I knew there never was a saint who'd led a happy life.

That was the trouble with Chrissy: happiness. I couldn't understand how she could come home from Lough Derg and sit at the kitchen table lightheartedly telling us about it, mimicking this one and ridiculing that, as though nothing had happened. The descriptions of the penances were enough to frighten me, never mind trying to imagine what size of sin demanded such expiation. And thinking that she might have been guilty of some heinous enormity cast a shadow over her for me, made her seem lost to me a little. I saw her as having contracted the spiritual equivalent of the great fear of the day, a spot on the lung. From now on she'd have to be very careful.

But listening to her blithely continue (her *pièce de résistance* was an imitation of someone either sneaking a cigarette or cadging a drag), I became more concerned for her. It struck me that, for her, the whole experience was not a solemn sobering. Her laughter, I greatly feared, meant that her contrition was imperfect. Couldn't she see that to be sin-free was to be grave and constant? Surely she could. Even I could see that. The evidence was all around us. Look at Mam. Look at any woman. Didn't the whole town, Chris, make you realize that you were too true to be good?

3

Christmas was good, thanks to midnight mass, and it was fun to run through three dead masses in a row on the Feast of All Souls, but the best times for serving were Missions and Easter.

Although they had none of Easter's liturgical novelty, Missions were exciting. For the two weeks they were on the town felt more alert. The air was tense, as on the day of an important hurling match. There was an air of people going purposefully about their business, the way they did on fair-days. And it seemed that all around there was the clandestine sibilance of the turning over of new leaves.

A Mission drew as many country people into town as a good fair, especially men, which was a sure sign that there was something to be got from it, since farmers didn't come to town except from necessity and in the hope of gain. These glowering, heavy-booted men bargained with Providence, their sins beside them like so many fluke-ridden sheep or incontinent calves.

It was because of the country people that services started at the annoying hour of eight in the evening. Missions being invariably summertime events – summer was the slackest time of the year, devotionally speaking – the people of the fields had to be given time to eat and spruce up before the three or four mile trek in. The annoying part was that for us youngsters, starting at eight meant there was no time to get a game going either before or afterwards.

To kill time we usually hung around the stalls. These were another way in which Missions resembled fairs. But fair-stalls were stocked with the best British padlocks and three-in-one penknives of brightest Ruhr streel, and were manned by apostles of Mammon, fast-talking Dubliners wearing signet rings and new-fangled nylon shirts who communicated such an air of modernity and confidence that you knew you couldn't trust them. Mission stallholders were quiet, unassuming men and women (the same as ourselves, as people liked to think), soberly dressed, serene smiles illuminating their simple faces as they waited impassively behind their little counters. This was another mark of their respectability, the fact that they had real stalls, with counters, canvas awnings and display shelves at the back, entirely different in tone and bearing from the fair-men's arrangement of battered crates in the back of a van.

Mission stalls did their best trade in holy pictures. There were two sizes, prayerbook and wall. St Joseph was easily the most popular subject. Usually he was depicted looking out over the viewer's shoulder (as though standing on a wall), a lily in his right hand. St Antony of Padua was popular too. He was one of the handiest of the saints: if you lost something and prayed to him, he'd find it for you. Youth had its own saints: Dominic Savio and Maria Goretti, both notorious for their purity.

Then there were statues. In this branch of business Our Lady led the field. Easy for her, of course, since she appeared in so many different liveries. Our Lady of Lourdes, of Guadeloupe, of Mount Carmel . . . . Runner-up in statue-sales was, surprisingly, Blessed Martin de Porres, the first Latin American to be beatified. The lesson of his status was, presumably, that there was hope for everyone – hence his popularity. Lastly there were the treasures, the rosaries that

111

had crucifixes with relics in them, the miraculous medals, the white prayerbooks with ornate, gold-looking locks attached to their sides which were considered ideal for little girls.

It says something for the mood generated by the Mission that nobody showed any curiosity about the stallholders. Only now does it occur to me to wonder who they were and where they came from and how they knew where to come. Perhaps the various preaching orders issued a calendar of Missions according to which the pedlars planned itineraries. Maybe these camp-followers were members of some lay order, their plaster figures and oleographic images a subtle descent to the vivid inarticulacy of the faithful's creed, against which the power of the preacher (his licence to speak) could be measured to his advantage. Or could the portable store have been a penance – all that packing and unpacking – imposed by some vindictively imaginative confessor?

We invariably had Redemptorists for our Mission. Our own clergy, who hired them, wouldn't have any others. They were right, no doubt: Jesuits would have talked over our heads, and certainly wouldn't have roared enough at us, and probably were in any case much too expensive. I have no idea what three Redemptorists for a fortnight cost, but I assume financial considerations were, as ever, to the fore in the minds of our pastors.

It was the thing that irked people most about the Church – money. There were collections for the Pope ('Peter's Pence') and for the Church ('Propagation of the Faith'). There were the various drives for parochial funds – whist drives, 45 drives; the collections at both Sunday masses, payment for mass cards, fees for official functions (baptisms, weddings). And above all there were dues, collected at Christmas and Easter in order that the clergy might pay their way. This contribution was the most difficult to avoid for the simple, though bizarre, reason that a list of donors plus amounts was read from the pulpit during mass a few Sundays after the take. Anyone who wanted to know how you were fixed economically, or if you were trying to curry clerical favour, or if you were trying to get above your station by flashing the wad, was given plenty to chew on. So was anyone who couldn't give a damn one way or the other. (No prizes for guessing which of those two parties was more numerous.) Moreover, the litany of names and numbers (from 'Doctor Healy £5' down to the rank and file, lumped together according to amount, 'Two shillings: Billy Mulcahy, Moses Kennedy . . . '), was often followed by a harangue about the necessity of supporting God's anointed, and we should never forget it. That Sunday we were all publicans, and we were all sinners.

Well, perhaps not all. Georgie, for one, was given to speaking his exasperated and cynical mind in reaction to such crass expressions of clerical thanks, muttering, 'never satisfied', 'bloody spongers'. And, warming to his theme, what, time after time, Geo wanted to know was: why did the three priests have a car each? 'One'd be plenty,' for reasons Geo would spell out in detail. Trailing after his vigorous resentment, though, was a sad thought about all he might accomplish if he could afford a car – sad, because it only made matters worse to be jealous of men to whom he was entirely indifferent to begin with. Resentment wasn't exclusive to Georgie, however. When the harangue was particularly importunate, Mam got annoyed too. Sometimes she even went as far as cutting her next contribution by a whole half-crown, from ten bob to seven-and-six (more she could not do: people'd start thinking us paupers).

Not all the sermons from our own men were demands for money with menaces. Father McGrath (not the Canon, but sandy-haired Father Dinny from Clashmore, who once expressed a great *grá* for me to Mam) was fond of exhorting us to be 'up and doing', and derived many striking variations from the text concerning he who is in the field – 'let him not turn his back for his coat.' Canon Walshe, I dimly remember, performed interminable exegetical callisthenics on the Good Samaritan, and also displayed a fascination with Samaria, which he pronounced 'Sam-mar-eye-a', making God only knows what connection between the Marian and the Roman province. 'Oh blessed hour!' Mam exclaimed, bustling in to put the kettle on, 'I thought he'd never shut up.'

Needless to say, however, no performance by a local could compare to an evening with a Redemptorist. They were the boys to lay it on hot and heavy, and on whose account we shivered in our shoes. Yet, squirming under the lash, I for one took pleasure in my guilt because I felt equipped with a stable identity, that of a sinner. I found that it concentrated the mind   113 wonderfully to have one's satanic tail hanging limp and decidedly unbushy between one's legs.

The themes of the sermons were chosen to appeal to various sections of the congregation. For children there was 'He went down to Nazareth and was subject to them'; for mothers, the prophecy of Simeon: 'And thine own soul a sword shall pierce'; for the men of the town: 'Do you not know that I must be about my father's business?' There were a few general ones as well. 'The gates of hell shall not prevail against it' introduced vigorous Commie-bashing. And 'Thou hast made us for thyself, O Lord, and our hearts are restless until they rest with thee' ('words taken, my dear brethren, from the great St Augustine') prefaced an unmerciful onslaught on the vanities of the world, in particular that laboratory of evil and illusory joy, company keeping.

The Missioners had two styles of delivery, loud and deafening. The deafeners often started out deceptively, sometimes even deigning to soften us up with a joke if they detected tension (and some evenings even we altar-boys could feel the electric expectancy of, say, a thousand souls waiting to be chastised). Here's a Redemptorist joke. 'A workman was wheeling a barrow of manure to the local lunatic asylum, and one of the lunatics was watching and watching him. At last the lunatic said, 'What's that for?' 'Oh,' said the workman, 'that's for the rhubarb'. 'Wisha, God love you,' said the lunatic, 'We get custard on ours.' There'd be a smattering of titters and sniggers, and sometimes a *sotto voce* repeat of the punchline: 'custard on ours . . . . In the name of the Father and Son and the Holy Ghost. Amen.' With the sign of the cross the lull ended and the storm commenced. Five minutes after the final simper had subsided, the winds of rhetoric, to quote the Paycock, 'blowed and blowed', making the rigging and frail fretwork of our immortal souls groan.

Reclining on the steps of the altar, facing the congregation, we servers felt like smug, safe insiders as we surveyed the looks of the miserable sinners. The preacher could pound the pulpit and shake his fist, his spittle could spray the front seat, but thanks to our position and our uniforms we knew ourselves to be basically on his side and immune from confrontation. The guilt I felt was inspired by loyalty to the occasion, not by any feeling of wrong-doing. Naturally we were closer to the

Missioners than anyone else in the town was – who attended to them in the first act of the day, after all?

And sometimes closeness didn't stop at serving their masses. I, for one, was fortunate enough to spend what I thought at the time was a perfectly wonderful afternoon in the company of a Father Carroll CSSR. It was great because we went on a walk together and I was able to assume my second-favourite role in the whole world, that of a guide – I used to drive my father mad in Dublin shouting out the names of the streets our bus was passing through. (My favourite role of all time was, of course, that of obedient child. But my assumption of it wasn't always voluntary or deliberate.) So for a while we strolled along and Father Carroll – my memory is of a somewhat fleshy man in his late twenties – asked me the usual boring questions about school, and was I a good boy at home, and was I better at football or hurling, to which I replied 'Yes, Father' and 'No, Father,' venturing such information as I imagined might interest him.

I'd have been quite satisfied if our walk had continued in this placid way. It wasn't what we said that mattered. The very idea of being in the exclusive company of such a holy man – a man so obviously superior to our own clergy, since he'd given up his whole life to wrestling the devil for souls and didn't own a car or anything – was plenty for impressionable me. But it made our afternoon really great when he told me that he might be going out foreign soon. Now that was *really* the thing . . . . It was all very well to fight the devil on your home ground. But to go out there looking for him in places where, from all I'd heard of pagany, he felt a lot more welcome – Boy!

Where was he going? I wanted to know, suddenly bold and free in my responses. Father Carroll didn't rightly know, but he thought they had the Philippines in mind for him. 'They're an awful long way away,' he said.

I know, I thought, aren't you lucky! I saw round-headed, oval-eyed children looking in awe at a man with a book. I saw a body of water filled with sampans and junks (vessels which I knew existed from the cover of *The Far East*, a periodical put out by another missionary order). I saw myself and Father Carroll cycling out from our adjoining parishes, all in white on shiny new bikes, sunlight and cool fronds beguiling us.

I ran home to tea with my head full of dreams. Georgie came

in from work as I was blurting it all out and asked what was up
with me. Starting all over again, which I was only happy to do,
wanting everyone to partake in my joy. I was taken aback only
to get as far as, 'I was out for a walk with the Missioner', before
Geo broke in roughly: 'Did you tell him about me?'

'Oh, I did,' said I, innocently.

'You'd a right to keep your bloody trap *shut*!' George cried.

'And so had you,' put in Mam, swiftly. 'Mouth almighty!'

I cried, of course, and cried again later when, tucking me in,
Chrissy told me Geo thought I'd told how bad a Catholic he
was. The second bout of tears was worse because I hated
George to think I'd let him down, and because it was awful to
imagine his soul in jeopardy (what if he fell from a ladder in
the morning?).

But neither tears nor Geo could eclipse entirely my new all-
white image of myself. Radiant with resolve, I wondered why
I hadn't thought of the foreign missions before. Was it because
I was weak and a cry-baby, and because I knew that God did
not require the services of somebody who was always falling
down and making his knees bleed? To love God as he
deserved demanded stamina – look at how healthy all the
priests I knew were. None of them looked like finicks with
their food. But now, fortified by the attentions of Filipinos, I'd
blossom forth in all sorts of exuberant, heroic ways. I'd be the
indefatigable instrument of the will of God, the eternal altar-
boy in unceasing attendance on my beloved, invisible celeb-
rant. I'd suffer the little picanninies to come unto me, as well,
and would only beat them if they were *very* saucy in school.

My vocation had me feeling extremely thankful, strangely
cleaned, and that nothing further would happen now to
damage me. I don't know how long these feelings would have
lasted in the normal course of events. But, as it happened, I
received a rude awakening, and from none other than the man
who'd converted me, Father Carroll himself.

Ever since our encounter I naturally absorbed his every
gesture, drank down his every word, and looked up to him as
much as I dared, which was nothing like as much as I wanted.
Less than a week later, however, we parted company. It was
lipstick that did it.

I forget now what text he used, probably Paul to the Corin-
116 thians: 'Your body is a temple of the Holy Ghost', but I

remember very well how scalding his remarks were. His main point struck me as pretty elementary: he objected to getting lipstick on his fingertips when he gave out communion. But why didn't he speak on mouth-opening as a prerequisite for wafer-reception? Because, no doubt, that would not have provided enough to rant and rave about. And did he ever! Women who composed themselves for the reception of their Lord and Saviour by wearing make-up were the worst in the world. How dare they improve their God-given features with powder and paint! They were no better than the leavings of London streets. Whited sepulchres, that's what they were. But God isn't fooled . . . .

He railed for a good hour, and long before he finished I was squirming. I thought of Chrissy. Sure she meant no harm with those creams and colourings. She only wanted to look nice and to be happy. There was no reason for Father Carroll to lose his temper with her, I said to myself – and then it dawned on me where my loyalties lay. Someone else could have the new bike and white soutane.

Now Passionists would never give a sermon like that. Of course they were different in every respect. They came from Mount Argus, in Dublin, pretty near where my father and Peggy lived in Sundrive Road, whereas the Redemptorists came from Limerick only (any place except Dublin and Cork was regarded as an enlarged and unimpressive Lismore). They looked different. Redemptorists dressed like the secular clergy. Passionists, however, while not going to the extreme of the sockless Cistercians, seemed definitely that way inclined. They never wore suits, only soutanes, they never appeared without their birettas, and they had big cloaks with Latin-inscribed, white pasteboard valentines stuck over their hearts: I always thought there was a touch of Zorro about them, and I laughed when Peggy said once, flippantly (to my ears, like a city person), 'Oh, the Passionate fathers with the loose habits'. But nobody else laughed. Everyone believed that the Passionists were the real thing. 'Saintly men,' said Mam, somewhat unctuously.

No doubt the reason why they were taken with a sizeable pinch of awe was because their narrow, intense mission – to preach the passion and death of Our Lord Jesus Christ. And   117

then they came at a very special time of the year, Easter –
though, with what seemed peculiar tact and self-denial, they
left the Resurrection alone. It was easier to take preachers
seriously at Easter, because it sounded like what they were
trying to do was normalize the extraordinary, not (like the
Redemptorists) lift up the mundane. They had great material
too – all that blood . . . .

And Easter was undoubtedly the best time in an altar-boy's
year. True we no longer had *Tenebrae*, as Mam boasted they
did in her day. (I listened, intrigued, as she described the
pitch-dark church and the clapping congregation – mimicry of
the chaos and ruin which were the immediate aftermath of the
Saviour's passing.) Still, we did all right as we were. There was
the shrouding of the statues in purple cerements; there was
the distribution of cool, chemical-smelling palm-leaves (actually sprigs of pine); there was the ordeal of lighting the thick,
naked-looking Paschal candle. We had no bell to ring, instead
we smacked a book. The tabernacle was vacated and left open,
so we had its cloth-of-gold lining to fascinate us. Devotions
took place at odd hours of the day (3 p.m. on Good Friday).
And we were off school.

The whole difference of it – the whole sense of the Church
putting itself out– seemed a reward for all the raw times of
Lent, when everyone tried to give things up and were grumpy
whether they succeeded or not, and adults were only allowed,
in the words of the bishop's instructions, 'One meal and two
collations' – a dietary prescription which was an indefensible
attack on the working man, according to Georgie. The names
of Easter – Pontius Pilate, Judas Iscariot, Annas and Caiphas,
Simon of Cyrene, Barabbas, the Sanhedrin – seemed some sort
of climax, coming all together, of the strange names of Lent:
Ash Wednesday, Quinquagesima, Rogation Days. And Easter
obliged us to live our faith in real time. Every day meant
something vital now – Spy Wednesday, Holy Thursday . . . .
None of the usual ticking-over from Sunday to Sunday. Faith
was a matter of concentration, intensity, cataclysm. For four
days Lismore was no longer a place where nothing ever
happened. It was a small world in a huge constellation bearing
witness to an agony which was its sole salvation. It was
eschatology, paradise for a people to whom a blend of politics,
law and bloodshed was mothers' milk.

The Passionists' sermons certainly helped to concentrate the mind wonderfully on redemptive agony. I don't remember very clearly the generalized exhortations and symbolical transformations with which the sermons concluded, possibly because they were pretty familiar. I knew already that every sin I committed was another thorn in the crown, another blow from 'the rude and scoffing soldiery'. And Peter's cock-crow denials didn't interest me a bit. What really got me involved were the thoroughly visceral sermons, the ones that went through the passion blow by blow, from Gethsemane to Golgotha, describing the medical pathology of the events. 'Did you ever hit your fingernail a blow with a hammer? (And did you ever take the name of Our Lord Jesus Christ in vain at the pain and shock of it?) Well consider, dearly beloved, what it might be like to hammer a nail into your hand. Not just a tack, but a big six-inch nail.' Or the hand would be described, its nerves, its moving parts, its delicate, God-designed tissue. 'Think what it would be to do that to your worst enemy. Then THINK what it was to PUNISH the SON OF GOD, who LOVES you!' There was another one too about the perversion of everyday things – timber and tools, for example – which struck me as highly ingenious, though it was no match for the technicolor gore efforts. There was nothing like them for instilling pity and awe, for reminding us (as our history so often tried to do) that the ultimate – or maybe even sole – test of good faith is self-abnegation. We don't stand a chance until we embody or articulate the nothingness that either our enemies or our own misdeeds have made of us. Talk about 'a terrible beauty . . .'.

What I understand even less, though, are the Easter Sundays. How it never rained on them. And, coming home from first mass, how mild as milk the air seemed, as gentle and beneficent as the breath of the risen Lord himself, wavering spring grown strong at last. Now there would be sugar in tea again, and cigarette packets snappily unwrapped. My father was here, and a week of walks with him lay delightfully in wait (I'd be able to tell him, for the umpteenth time, the story of my favourite picture, *The Crimson Pirate* – Burt Lancaster and Nicky Cravat: maybe this time he'll be impressed). In the wings, of course, were profound miracles which I never took the slightest bit of notice of – birdsong, daffodils. And trifle for afters.

V

THE CLASH OF THE ASH

1

'Look at that, Seoirse,' said Chrissy. 'Show him, George.'

Painfully, Georgie rolled up a leg of his trousers.

'Look.'

I saw a mass of bruise, blue, black, smoke-yellow, red-edged.

'What happened?' I said, alarmed, but I already knew. Indeed, without realizing it, I'd seen it happen. Georgie had been hurling.

It was a junior match between ourselves and Kilgobnet, a crowd of savages from down the county (the opposition always consisted of savages). Georgie was our full-back. Every time the ball came into the square their full forward pulled across him, hit him with the boss of the hurley. He was a ruffianly, dirty scut, so he was, as the spectators' growls confirmed. But what he was doing was entirely commonplace. Lismore's poor record in the county championship during those years was partly due to our not having enough players prepared to 'stick into' their opposite numbers. I was not surprised by what I'd seen on the field. What startled me was the sight of the mottled leg and the realization that hurling had an aftermath. Before then I'd always imagined that whatever happened, even the blood that I'd frequently seen flow, was all play and was absorbed by, or abandoned to, the field when the match ended. Sunday's exploits were in a class of their own, to me; it was unsettling to learn that they might be accompanied by Monday's aches.

George squirmed as he rolled down his trouser-leg. 'That sonofabitch,' he said. 'I'll get him the next time.' And he stumped off out to work.

I felt sorry for him. It wasn't right. The ref was a louser. 123

Nobody was for Lismore. But underneath my sympathy I felt relief. Maybe it was all for the best that I was a useless hurler.

I wanted to be a star, of course. I yearned to tear away on a blistering solo-run, to send bullets into the back of the net, to exemplify 'the finer points of the game' and the art of 'bending, lifting and striking' which brought headlong Michael O'Hehir to hysteria on the radio. And some cheering crowds, a gold medal or two, and my picture in the paper would, I believed, have done me no harm at all.

Being by birth a Wexford-man (a 'yellow-belly'; Georgie used to tease me with the Wexford nickname, which I found very upsetting, feeling that I was being made a stranger), I had plenty to nourish my dreams of derring-do. At that time, Wexford had a wonderful team – though typical of one that I supported it never won as much as it should have. It had the three Rackards – powerful Nick up front, staunch Bobby defending, subtle Billy in mid-field. It had Ned Wheeler with the blond hair, Art Foley the goalie who stopped raspers with a minimum of show, Padge Kehoe who was either the son or nephew of some famous friend of my Uncle Seamus. A few of these heroes were even from my birth-place, Enniscorthy, a fact I found very thrilling, it being more proof of my specialness.

Neither my own appetite nor the achievements of my mother's county made a hurler of me, however. I was, unalterably, all fantasy and no execution. I had no stomach whatsoever for taking the field, stick in hand – and so lightly clad! On the contrary, I knew all too well that I was too frail and too afraid for the hue-and-cry of it all.

My frailty was something I was much more aware of than my fear. Mam told me all about it: how pale and peaky I'd been, how for nights on end she'd be by my bedside, how there was always a nice drop of Scotch broth simmering in case I unexpectedly found an appetite.

'Ah,' she'd reminisce fondly, 'Dad [my grandfather] used to say, You'll never do it. He'll never last. Oh, he will, I'd say. I'll pull him through. And I did.'

Her talk gave me a typical picture of myself. I was in a narrow bed; my face was as white as a sheet; my wan smile is struggling gamely against listlessness; adults are whispering together in a corner. I am pitiable and unlikely. I have been chosen by the same imponderable agencies as those to which my poor mother succumbed. I am being tested by God. The metaphysics of my complaint were more enervating than the complaint itself. I must have been the world's worst patient. Illness made me frail, no doubt, but so too did the long bouts of convalescence which followed. Even after the merest quinsy Mam and Chrissy watched me as though I was on the point of evaporating.

With such great care being taken of me, I was extra careful to take good care of myself. In the playground I hung well back from the rough and tumble. When anyone came near me I fell down and cut my knee and had a bandage, lint and boric powder applied to it as soon as I got home. (I fell down at the hint of roughness as promptly as I cried at the sound of harsh words. It was an excellent stratagem, releasing me from numerous nervous situations for the expense of just a little blood. But as with the tears, the falls came unplanned.) When I played hurling I stood with my stick around mid-field near the sideline, and prayed the ball wouldn't come near me. It usually didn't, thank God; it whizzed by, pursued by a thunder of big-fellows, gasping and snorting, pulling and hooking. 'The clash of the ash!' That was a sound (and a phrase) meant to kindle the spirits of all right-thinking Irishmen, but it left me cowering.

It was some consolation to realize that I didn't have to be a Cuchullain with stick and ball to prove my Irishness. In fact, I firmly believe that Irishness was my one unimpeachable attribute, which no amount of mere personal incompetence could diminish. The reason for this unwonted security was my mother. Thanks to her I had a splendidly patriotic lineage, one so pristine that it totally outshone anything Lismore could boast of. I didn't boast, of course: I just felt smug.

My mother's father, Liam Royce, had fought in 1916, not in Dublin, but even more abortively in Enniscorthy. Her mother served in Cumann na mBan. They were married in traditional dress, he in a kilt and tunic, she in green with *brat* attached by a Tara brooch, and a piper had played at the wedding. They learned Irish. They studied manuals of cavalry warfare. They were going to change the world. And two young men who were to become Mammy's uncles were with them, and rose out as well, when the time came. All Uncle Mike got for his 125 efforts was a bit of his thumb shot off. But Uncle Seamus did better. When I knew him he was a morose man who wanted nothing more from life than the power to eliminate black spot, green fly and all the other natural shocks which beset roses. A far cry from the time when he was an insurance clerk by day and a conspirator at night. (My sense of him is that the piquant paradox of that combination never crossed his mind.)

He was fairly famous, though. I could never quite understand why. The achievement of anybody who hadn't been executed was obscure to me. But I know that, along with his comrades, he suffered in Frongoch Camp. And when he was released from there he became a member of the first Dáil, and a lifelong friend of de Valera.

The last bit was what impressed Mam, herself 'mad Dev' (as she said) 'ever and always'. This was not a popular position in Lismore, but Mam prided herself on it. She admired Dev's stiffness, his ability at sums, his answer to Churchill at the end of the last war, his guts for sticking to his guns with his back to the wall. She also admired his spectacles. For her they were arguably his most important feature, lending his face a clerkly chastity and inwardness. Nothing of the foreigner's roast-beef floridity of feature about him, nor yet was he disgraced by nature in the manner of his mallet-skulled, bullet-headed, pig-visaged opponents. (When it came to chastising enemies Mam was an inspired exponent of the cephalic index.) On top of which – bonus of bonuses! – Dev's glasses made him seem kin to that other bespectacled arbiter of Mam's known world, Pius XII.

Dev came to Lismore once, electioneering. He stood on the back of Dowd's lorry and harangued a fair-sized crowd for half-an-hour. I remember it being an evening meeting, one of perhaps half a dozen whistle-stops he made in the long dusk when men were in from the fields. I remember the strange energy of a stimulated crowd dispersing, and a moon-faced labourer wearing a beret and with slight slope to his walk shouting 'Up Dev!' as he made off up Chapel Street home to Ballinaspick. I remember Dev as something all the family agreed on. So Mam was very proud of being able to claim proximity to her hero through my Uncle Seamus. It was a vindication of her politics that her eldest son married into lofty principles, gunfire and near-martyrdom, though a more gentle, mild-mannered group of people than my mother's family I find it hard to imagine.

Mam would have taken good care of it that I was proud of them too, supposing I didn't feel that way inclined. I had no problem, however, identifying with them and their romantic, obscure, triumphant past. Whatever it was they were trying to bring about – of course I knew quite well what their historical and political attainments were; what I couldn't quite grasp was that the boyish spirit of their efforts had not been sustained; their day was a lot more exciting than mine, which though intriguing I thought unfair – at least they hadn't shirked it, whereas in Lismore nobody knew what was going on until it was all over. I discriminated unfairly, irrelevantly, between Lismore and almost the whole of the rest of the country outside Dublin. But pride in my patriots also acted as another reminder that I wasn't where I should be. I should be living among the Notables and Elders of the Cause on the banks of the quick-silvery Slaney. The shadow of their history should fall, transformingly, on me.

When I visited Enniscorthy, however, I was not changed utterly. Indeed in some ways, my sense of frailty was reinforced. Granny Royce and I would be walking home from the L & N with a teatime treat when, going by the convent, a neighbour would stop and after a few pleasantries say, 'Oh, and this is Nuala's little chap,' at which Nuala's mother would blink fondly, tearfully, and I would meet myself once more as a refugee from death. 'By the gob o' man, missus, he's gone as big as a house,' Paddy Nolan might say from behind his counter in Rafter Street. And although he spoke merrily, I always felt my existence surprised him.

Paddy always treated me to a bottle of Lett's lemonade, however, which quickly made me feel again a chosen person in a positive sense, something the Donaghues accomplished much more adeptly. Whenever I was taken into their shop I was given ice-cream immediately and never felt a thing, even though just across dark, narrow Slaney Street from them stood the house I was born in. They never said a thing. Sim came out to shake hands with me, thrusting forward his red-brick, owl-oval, eyebrow-free face at me. His large wife remained behind the counter, her placid smile like a dent in a firkin of butter.

I looked upon the lemonade and ice-cream and saw that 127

they were good (and that they were no more than my due). I also saw them as being a kindly tribute to a respected local, Granny Royce. So in that way, too, I felt nearer to my desire for specialness, for recognition as a breed apart. Additional assistance came from the unfamiliar accents on the streets, flatter, with quaint usages and asseverations such as 'Ain't it' and 'Be the tear!' And of course there was a different history. The castle in Enniscorthy is on the side of the street, commanding nothing. Much more eye-catching is the statue of the man with the pike in the middle of the square. The countryside's main landmark was not some imperial implant but a place where the have-not peasantry was ruined in 1798, Vinegar Hill, a bleak bump of a place that glowered at the town below. A history consisting of the wasteful death of humble people was one with which I could identify.

The desired ratification did not take place, however. Enniscorthy did not take me to its heart. I remained a novelty passing through. While the place seemed a tissue of redactions of my history, I was the only one aware of it. Nobody else had the need, I suppose. Their need was to be absolved of history, not to claim it. This strikes me as being especially true of my two heroic uncles. Seamus had a fortification of roses. Uncle Mike owned a hardware shop and was radio-mad. Neither of them ever offered anything of his history to me. The very thing that lent them substance, mystery, power and manhood – in my eyes – was the very thing they had effaced. I never wanted to prompt them into volunteering a tale or two. That would break the spell of desire. So they never did. There seemed to be no relief from the sense that we were all living in an aftermath, a limbo. I could be as Irish as I wanted. The degree was irrelevant. The condition of Irishness didn't apply. When I went back to Lismore I still had to try and prove myself hurling. I was the same as everyone else, after all, a person without alternatives.

Every Friday afternoon, to end the week, Brother Blake would lead most of the primary school out from the monastery, along the Tallow road, in past Dunne's lodge and along the Castle farm-track to the field (rented by the hurling club from the Castle). To him it was a great outing. Once off the main road, and out of the Brother Superior's hearing, he'd burst into song: 'I love to go a-wandering', usually, though he had a good 'Gipsy Rover' as well. He could croon quite well in his thick Clare accent, and would shout at us to join in the chorus. We'd go:

> Awdi-du, awdi-du aw day
> Awdi-du, awdi-day-dee
> He whistled and sang till the green woods rang,
> And he won the heart of a lady.

Once at the field he'd appoint captains and have them pick teams. Captains were usually favourites; either Blakey was a friend of the family or the lad was good in class or he was just a pet and a good hurler. If I'd been able to hurl I'd have been well set for captaincy, because Blakey had taught with my father in Dublin before being shifted to Lismore, and had come to tea one Christmas for a chat about old times with him. And didn't Mam and all the brothers meet every morning at convent mass? So by rights I should be given some sort of prominence. But I was never a favourite of his. It wasn't I he called 'ceann bán' and put his arm around, but Leonard Lyons of Botany. The only thing he did for me was give me permission to go to the lavatory whenever I wanted to without raising my hand. I had to go a lot.

Although there were enough of us to make a reasonable number of seven-a-side teams, the invariable format was to divide us into two factions, town and country. This was done in order to foster competition, which was the thing Brother Blake liked to do best. In class – he had the three junior primary classes; Brother Murphy the two senior – he also divided us up, naming the teams after parts of the town and awarding points for scholastic attainment (in sums, spelling and writing), while deducting them for bad behaviour and stupid mistakes. Around three o'clock every day the schoolroom atmosphere (the three classes were in the one room) was a fine old frenzy of nerves as the competition reached its climax, since whichever team won couldn't be caned the following day. Winning was a wonderful feeling, almost as good as making a mistake next day and realizing Blakey couldn't beat you for it.

Dividing us into town and country teams was shrewd and

pointed. Any other division would have struck us as weak and artificial. But nobody felt that Blakey was imposing a rivalry by having us compete along community lines. The antagonism was already there. It wasn't necessarily clear-cut, however. Most of us townies had farmers' sons as friends, and regarded some of them as just about our equals. But localized exceptions didn't affect the general outlook. We despised the country and all belonging to it, and felt ourselves immeasurably superior to everything it stood for.

Town was a world of its own, independent, aloof: no cowshit, no pig-squeals, no thatch. Town was cinemas, shops, priests and policemen. It didn't take a genius to work out where the world would be without any of them. The country was all tearing and dragging. It was weather-watching, chores at sunrise, accents sounding like gravel being shovelled. And country lads (*cabógs*, we called them) were no good in school, slow, dull, humourless, sullenly and silently objecting to book-work, sensing no doubt that they had no need of it, but were merely in attendance out of legal obligation, only to be beaten for being so obliging – well, why should they bother, wasn't there land ever before books were thought of? Most of them quit after primary school, an odd few going on to do the Intermediate Certificate, a rare one or two finishing secondary.

They, in turn, thought us weaklings, cissies, Mammies' boys, half-men who'd never pulled a teat, choked a chicken, or forked a bale of hay. They had arcane jokes. 'How d'you get down off a donkey? You don't, you get down off a duck.' Their breath smelled of buttermilk, slightly raw and unsavoury, and they had to walk miles to get anywhere. But, as tradition decreed, they had the brawn right enough. They were fitter and stronger and ran rings around us. They seemed easier to please, too. Perhaps getting together to play was a greater novelty for them, or maybe showing their paces was. At any rate, they overran us, while we stood around frustrated and complained of being fouled, the brains which tradition said we possessed as useless to us as swatches of wet straw.

Blakey loved the whole thing. He ran up and down, in a gloating, giggling gargle and roaring hoarse encouragement – always in Irish, a vain effort to bring the national tongue down to the everyday level of the national game. It wasn't that anybody objected to Blakey using such phrases. The practice lent him novelty, and therefore a certain amount of credibility, as a teacher, the way singing 'Val-de-ree, Val-de-raw' going to the field did. Gaels were not so common amongst us that we could take their behaviour for granted. Moreover, as Mam told me, being from Clare Brother Blake was not only Gaelic but 'mad Dev' as well, that was 'only natural' for a native of what Blakey himself called, proudly if obscurely, 'the Banner County'. I knew I was supposed to be impressed by the Irish-Dev connection, but if it did indeed confer an honoured place in Gaeldom on its beneficiaries, why was the Clare county team as useless at hurling as our own? This deficiency worried me: surely everything was supposed to interlock – hurling, Irish, Dev, God, the O'Briens and me?

That kind of worry was a luxury, of course, an exercise, a combination of conundrum and eye-opener. Much more pressing, and just as strange, was the way Blakey relished the country lads' triumphs. Monday morning, first thing after the prayer, he'd write the score up on the board. *An tuath 3-5, an baile 1-2. Ar aghaidh an tuath!* Oh, it was mortifying: those louts getting the best of us. Well next Friday – you could hear the intolerance seethe around the room – we'll knock 'em into kingdom come. For five or ten minutes even I felt ashamed of my inability, and I longed for nothing better than to hammer the country single-handed with unprecedented feats of stick-work.

Being a hopeless hurler made me ashamed in a more complex way too, however. It made me lie to Georgie.

'How'd you get on, Mike?' he'd ask at tea.

'Okay,' sheepishly.

'Did you score?'

'A goal and a point,' heart hammering.

'Good on you. Did ye win?'

'Naw,' with immense relief, though all disguised.

I thought to tell the truth would be a greater offence. My athletic incompetence was, I felt, a species of disloyalty to him and all he'd done for me – made me hurleys, bought me balls, brought me to matches – as well as all he stood for, his sideboard silver and his beaten leg.

And then, as well, I had to lie to protect myself. If I told him how I really was I felt sure he'd shout and carry on at me and 131 give me useless advice. 'Arra what ails you? Don't mind anyone. Wade in there. You'll do fine. And if anyone's too rough, just tell me.' It wasn't possible to say, 'I can't.' I couldn't be different from him. He loved me too much to allow it. So I lied. And he let me. Week after week I gave him a false tally. He never questioned it. Never even asked for the details for which the bare figures were such a transparent substitute. My lies were punished by his indulgent trust.

I found myself in the thick of the action once. Noel Coffey was going to strike an almighty blow for the opposition.

'Hook him. Hook him!' was the cry.

So I put my hurley in front of his as he was about to come out of his backswing, and sure enough he missed the ball.

Instead he knocked me cold for maybe as much as ten seconds. When I came to, I was 'spouting' from a cut over the eye. The sky was full of faces. There was a lot of jabbering. Nobody knew what to do. I was helped up and someone was told to escort me as far as the monastery kitchen where Nora, the housekeeper, washed me off and told me to call into Mr Hanrahan on the way home to find out if I needed a stitch. A stitch! Marvellous martyrdom by catgut and needle!

Using strips of tape, however, Mr Hanrahan deprived me, and even seemed to enjoy his ingenuity. Still, when I did get home, there was a gratifying outburst 'Oh my God!' and 'Sit down, boy', and questions galore. Mam went, 'Coffey . . . Coffey . . . ', narrowing her eyes, but she couldn't come up with anything to blacken the name of Noel or his people. So she just reassured me that 'them fellas' were all too big and rough for me, and I felt that my weakness was in a way precious to her, and that maybe I'd be sent to bed with hot lemonade.

I wasn't. Worse yet, when Georgie came home, he only threw me, 'Thing o' nothing. It'll make a man o' ya.' How much more face could my injury lose? I was looking forward to tons of attention, and I just knew I'd have to stay off school because every time I hung my head a little blood seeped from the cut. But by the Sunday I was well enough to write to my father about it, and by Monday I was back tackling vulgar fractions as though nothing had happened. In fact, the most memorable aspect of the whole affair was my father's letter back, in which he said I was becoming 'a war-scarred veteran'.

This strange phrase (he was not given to toughening me up to be his manly little soldier or anything like that) struck me as pleasantly sympathetic, with its fancy ring. It wasn't all that easy to pronounce, but it had an obvious truth to it which appealed. I had been in the wars. Then, as I savoured it, the phrase revealed a deeper meaning to me, a connection between hurling, battling and bloodshed which I was easily able to manipulate into a sense of patriotic self-congratulation. I too had suffered for my Irishness. Now I belonged with my mother's people, belonged more irrevocably than if, with open arms, they'd made me theirs.

It fell to Mam, however, to demonstrate exactly what such a sense of belonging could entail. And it came out of nowhere, that searing testament of hers, out of no more than Pa Sheehan's innocuous, light-hearted, weekly visit.

We all loved Pa. He was an agent for Royal Liver Insurance, a queer-seeming company to me, because it had a cock for a mascot. Up hill and down dale Pa travelled, collecting dues for them in his black Volks. 'Greatest car ever made,' he asserted vigorously, his Tallow accent rattling along like coal down a chute.

Pa was short, rotund, and very jolly. The adults loved him because he brought in all the news, tales of who might die next, who was on the mend, who was fighting, who was courting. He mimicked backsliding clients for us, speculated about lawsuits, overstayed his welcome by an hour or more, supping tea and sucking cigarettes.

And Mam was fond of Pa too, because he embodied pleasant memories. He had been a wonderful hurler in his day. If I'm not mistaken he won no less than an All-Ireland medal as a member of the first Waterford team to go all the way in the national championship. That was in 1948, and the twinkling pace of his manner now was reminiscent of the wit and speed that made him, as Mam said, 'like an ellet' when he played.

Anyhow, one Monday evening, in the casual drift of gossip, Pa mentioned something he'd heard about the organization of a Lismore soccer team. This had not been attempted before. The town did have a cricket team and those who turned out for it were considered by Mam to be beneath contempt, traitors to the race, 'shoneens'. The same labels were attached to anyone 133 who played any 'foreign game', licence to do so being implicitly provided by the rules of the Gaelic Athletic Association. So, I expected an outburst from Mam denouncing soccer. In fact I'd heard some of it before: soccer was a cissy's game, all tip-tap, no lavish scoring, played solely by cockney slum-dwellers and suchlike reprobates, for whom there was nothing deviant in the denial of hands. And in addition, now, those whose names Pa'd mentioned were idle *cadets*, useless articles, namby-pambies, deficient in unspecified yet definitive areas for declining to take swipes at one another with hard sticks.

'Well I don't know,' said Pa, mildly. 'I don't care what they're doing as long as it's not standing at the Red House corner waiting for something to happen.'

'Pa,' said Mam, vaguely alarmed, 'I'm surprised at you.'

'Ah, that oul' ban,' said Pa, referring to the GAA's prohibitions. 'Bad blood is all it ever caused. Of all things for people to be falling out over. They ought to get rid of it.'

'What?' cried Mam, huffily. 'After boys giving their lives, and that crowd trying everything they could to stop everything Irish, flamming the hands off in school if we spoke a word of our own language . . . . '

'I know all that, sure,' Pa said patiently. 'But listen. If Georgie or the child's father walked in the door and told you they were going to play soccer from this on, what would you do?'

'I'd show 'em the door,' said Mam harshly.

'You would not,' said Pa, gently dismissive.

'Oh, I would!' said Mam, bristling. 'I wouldn't have 'em under the same roof as me.'

'Your own flesh and blood?'

'Yes!'

'By gor,' said Pa, sighing, allowing his gaze to follow the flight of his cigarette butt to the fireplace, 'you're a hard woman.'

And she certainly looked it. Her face was as sheer and obdurate as steel, and as unflinching. It was a face that didn't have another cheek to turn. A face that was a prayer of dedication to the one true cause, to the only cause that had ever won through. Uncompromising, exalted, vindictive, extreme.

134 Irish.

I felt embarrassed. I felt sorry for Pa (he'd lost). I felt somehow weakened, confused, as though I'd been left standing bleakly alone, my hurley and its heritage reduced to a withered twig because I couldn't play.

2

As she probably knew, Mam had no reason to doubt Georgie's attachment to our national games. My father was a more likely source of concern. A nippy half-forward in his day – so I heard; as with so much about him I only have casual remarks to go on – he now spent all his free time going to foreign films. But Mam accepted as best she could that strange developments occur in cities. He hadn't stooped to foreign games, anyhow, thank God!

To call Georgie's involvement with the GAA that of a mere fan would be to misrepresent grievously its ardour. What went on between them was more like a marriage, tense, erratic, satisfying only in consummation (not in consciousness). Player, official, aspiring bureaucrat – or, if you like, lover, husband, self-styled head-of-household – there was no phase of the organization's activities in which he wasn't utterly, selflessly, critically engrossed.

He was past his prime as a player when I saw him. Full-back was his position, and no doubt he was what the papers call 'a stalwarth', often exhibiting 'tenacious defence' and 'clearing his lines with dispatch' (where did they get the pseudo-military lingo?), but more often shoving and poking and being beaten for speed. For me, too, there was an additional problem with the full-back position: it wasn't glamorous. Not for Geo the elegant overhead 'double', the point exquisitely picked off from an acute angle on the wing, the bullet scorching its way to the back of the net. Occasionally he might burst out of a ruck of enemies and deliver what the parlance called 'a long, relieving clearance'. But I wanted everything he did to be spectacular, lyrical, cheer-worthy. It was difficult to be stylish, I knew 135 that, I'd heard players being criticized for it: style was light-weight, aggression was what counted. I was disappointed, though, that Georgie couldn't, just once in a while, describe an exhilarating arabesque with his stick, or side-step musclebound intimidation, or beat an opponent to the pull with zesty speed. Why couldn't he be like Chrissy a little?

I wasn't too critical, however, because I could see what a good Gael he was in other respects, what a dutiful caretaker, loyal husband, diligent *domestique*. He could never do enough. On the day of a match he lined the pitch, which meant going around the field (110 yards by 30) with a brush and a bucket of whitewash, marking the boundary of the playing area. He painted the goal posts. He made the corner flags and the side-line flags and the flags for the umpires. He brought home the team's reeking jerseys and demanded they be washed, causing consternation among the two women, who neverthe-less scrubbed away, for all their mutinous mutterings, as though their sense of duty too was bound up in the black-and-amber of Lismore.

Georgie served unpaid, and largely unthanked, his sole reward an occasional senior county championship fixture or, more rarely, an inter-county exhibition game. The whole town feasted on the prestige and publicity of such events, and naturally George was thrilled to see the town, the club and the field recognized, though no doubt he would have slaved away regardless of whether a big match ever came to town or not.

I looked back with awe at his powers of commitment, at how fervently – and with enviable innocence – he believed that life is the possibility of total immersion. His involvement with the GAA was such that it went well beyond the narrow righteous-ness of national games. It had to do with activity as authentic-ity, with large-lifeness, with trying as hard as possible to obtain as much as possible on behalf of comradeship and community. Trying too hard, perhaps. I wouldn't be at all surprised to learn that other club members were less active than they wanted to be because of Geo's drive. But at the time it was very clear that nobody needed the outlet as badly as George. And it may be too that, thanks to being vulnerable in ways that other men his age had been able to grow out of,

136 Georgie was best placed to appreciate what the GAA

represented. It was the only secular, nationwide organization that offered a life larger than the everyday – the life of a designated, and perhaps archetypal, cultural participant, in which sinew surpassed cash-box, wind bettered prayer, body smote body playfully, and a crowd might still marvel. And a big match was not a small reward. It was wonderful to feel the streets filled with anticipation, to be borne along to the field by a garrulous throng. The sense of everyone enthusiastically united, which gave rise to the exhilarating notion that we were absolutely right to be carrying on as we were, made a match seem the thing for which mass was a rehearsal.

The Mellary Pipers Band would be in attendance. We'd all stand exuberantly to attention, face the tricolour and give out the national anthem. 'Soldiers are we . . . '. And who amongst us didn't feel that indeed he was? And just to make sure that this was an occasion, that living hallmark of the great day, the fiddler, turned up as well. Where he came from, and where he went to, nobody was able to tell me: it was as though the atmosphere had contrived him out of nowhere, in order to reproduce itself in his delirious reels. He got paid, too, I noted jealously. Not a man passed but didn't drop a copper or two into the little bag hanging from one of the tuning-pegs. (Women were stingier.) He'd nod his head thankingly, his elbow unceasing. His face was as brown as a nut.

Big matches had drawbacks, though. The crowds were so large, sometimes, and so avaricious for a glimpse of a star – Pad Stakelum of Tipperary, Philly Grimes of Mount Sion and Waterford, Duck Whelan of Abbeyside – that a nipper like me could hardly see a thing. I didn't mind that too much. The atmosphere was so charged it was hard to concentrate anyhow, and I was happier expressing my excitement by darting round the grown-ups' legs. Sometimes, too, dodging around, I'd run into Chrissy talking to some strange fellow (big matches were a fairly rare opportunity for girls to parade their finery), and I'd tug on her dress till she thrust a penny at me, scowling, 'Don't be so saucy!' and off I'd run to buy a Pixie bar or a Cough-No-More (the *jalapeño* of liquorice treats). God knows how many dates I may have ruined on her, how many hopeful swains drew back, thinking me a euphemistic nephew, thinking maybe that they had a lucky escape from the clutches of a fast woman as, after the game, they cycled   137 uphill home to milk the cattle.

The bad thing that big matches did was to reveal the field's inadequate facilities and to suggest, to me at any rate, that no matter how much Georgie might do it was never enough. The crowds showed that it was inconvenient to have a pee. What passed for a toilet was a few strips of whitewashed galvanized iron, behind which men could go. There were always too many waiting, though – predictably: who in his right mind would think of attending the centrepiece of his Sunday without a feed of porter? But I didn't like hopping from foot to foot in a thicket of hairy jackets and brown boots.

Also, the field had no changing-rooms. There was nothing unusual in that – no field had: the nearest ones were in the city of Cork. It was one thing, however, for veterans of local junior games to 'tog on' under the stand of limes behind the town goal, quite another for a luminary whose picture had been splashed in the *Independent* the previous week, especially as such demi-gods went in for new-fashioned shirts, that opened all the way down. It didn't seem right to me that they should be to the same rough-and-ready conditions as any yob from Knockanore or Gaultier.

Yet it was those very buckoes who provided the field's standard fare, barrel-chested swashbucklers from the back of beyond. Theirs was no flattery. They feelingly persuaded us what we were. If the big match embodied for us the lyric of carnival, the typical encounter enacted the drama of blood-feud. And their usages could be damn ugly. At these junior matches (junior and senior are categories of excellence, not age) the crowd was split and hostile. It generally wasn't satisfied to watch the action, it had to join in as well, invading the pitch and laying about them while club officials, among them usually a young curate, ineffectually went, 'Boys, Boys . . . '.

Some clubs were notorious. The Geraldines. Ballyduff. The Shamrocks. The rate at which they tore and slashed was simply terrifying. Nearly everyone in Lismore was too well-reared to fight, too respectable for that kind of thing. Besides, many were shopkeepers and reluctant to risk trade and reputation by allowing tempers to fray. If Lismore was too civilized to defend itself, the others (whoever they might be) were just out-and-out savages. The latter verdict kept the town honour intact. I suppose I subscribed to that outlook. Let the art of the

138

stick prevail, not the force of the arm. And at home I received repeated cautions from both Mam and Chrissy about unseemly, ruffianly fisticuffs.

Still, people continued to get hurt. George, of course. And I remember distinctly seeing a player for Brickey Rangers with one side of his face a bright red veil of blood. And I was at the field the Sunday Wally was stretchered off. That was the incident that really frightened me, because Wally was a neighbour and he nearly died.

It happened in a game of quite commonplace vehemence. The opposition was Fourmilewater, a team from the hills north of Dungarvan. Although he lived virtually next door to us, Wally lined out for the team nearest his own townland; he came from Camphire, so he played for Tourin. Such fidelity was entirely normal. For countrymen who'd newly settled or who had jobs in town, playing with their own sort was the only conceivable choice. So there was Wally at midfield in the pink-and-white stripes of Tourin, pulling across his opposite number every time the ball came near them – overhead, on the ground, every way – with his opposite number giving as good as he got, bits of broken hurley flying furiously out from them with every contact, to the cheers of the crowd, until at length down Wally went, and the crowd kicked up blood and murder.

Wally bled. He bled all the way to the doctor. The doctor advised immediate removal to the hospital in Dungarvan. He bled, we heard, the whole of that fifteen-mile drive. They didn't like the look of him in Dungarvan, so off to Ardkeen in Waterford City he went, still bleeding, for all I know, since by the time scraps of hearsay came my way Wally was virtually a man in a legend. 'Main strong,' people said, their tones a mixture of horror and admiration. 'If that was a town-boy, now, 'tis in a box he'd be.' But box-wards Wally seemed to drift: the next thing we knew he was up in the Richmond Hospital, Dublin, to have his skull operated on. Apparently a splinter from his opponent's stick had embedded itself – so I heard, anyhow. (Or maybe so I was told to stop me asking endless questions. Or maybe that's how legend had it afterwards, registering the force of the skull-opening blow.) I remember trying to picture the big knife, and shivering.

I remember, too, Georgie's forceful reactions, mainly   139 directed against the hurling bureaucracy. Why wasn't it compulsory for clubs to insure players? Even when Wally came home he still wouldn't be fit to work: what were his wife and child supposed to live on? Geo waxed highly indignant and disgusted, as though only realizing for the first time the inadequacies of amateurism and that hurling was really only a game, not an ethic. What were *they* doing about Wally? Bugger-all! Eventually, a benefit dance was held, but it took so long to organize that Wally may even have been home for it.

He did come home, I'm delighted to say. It was strange seeing him, his shaved head and ice-coloured face. Convalescing, he'd stand for an hour outside his front door and my friend Pete and I would stop and chat with him. His scar was plain to see, a livid snake of a thing that ascended from behind his right ear. He had a slightly crackling laugh. He spoke softly and obsessively about women. Six months passed. He went back to work for Hyde the timberman, pottering about. Main strong!

Chrissy and Mam agreed that Georgie's criticism of how Gaeldom handled the injury was nothing but the truth. His judgments were as quick and as definitive as Mam's. And the object of his criticism was familiar too. On winter Sundays, as the Lismore delegate, he attended meetings of various boards and councils, and on his return insisted on regaling us with examples of their idiocies and timidities, eyes turbid with Guinness and a cigarette cocked crookedly between marshy lips.

Geo never took me to these confabulations, no doubt aware of how bored I'd be, and I didn't mind much at the time, though I'm sorry now that I never heard him denounce in public, to their faces, the sub-clergy who ran the GAA. What I was sorry and very resentful about then was not being taken to the inter-county games at which he officiated. In vain, George tried to explain that he couldn't umpire effectively and keep an eye on me at the same time. I had no use for explanations predicated on responsibility; I'd heard too many of them. Nothing could persuade me that Georgie's having a day out without me wasn't the height of injustice. And not just any old day out either. The games he inspired were of championship significance; they'd be written up in the morning's paper. He was going to see Buttevant, Thurles, Kilmallock, towns which my sulking mind translated as Isfahan, Baghdad,

Constantinople.

It was an act of rank ingratitude for me to sulk (and I'm sure I cried a time or two as well: the slightest hint of being left out or being left behind was quite enough to start me off). As Mam impatiently reminded me, I'd no right to whine, Geo did damn well by me (implying, too well) – what about all the other days out I'd had with him? And at the mention of those, though I may have added a snivel or two for form's sake, I basically shut up. Mam was absolutely right, I couldn't deny it, there wasn't a child in the town who'd had more outings than me. And of all the good times of my childhood, those small excursions were without a doubt the best.

Cappoquin (four miles to the east) was the usual venue for Lismore's away fixtures. The distance didn't matter; I already felt transported thanks to the novelty of a car-ride. And I liked Cappoquin, even though Lismore people generally thought it a hole. That was because it had no scenery, the Blackwater just made an impressively wide right-angle turn to the sea there. Instead of a castle all it could boast of was a bacon factory. On weekdays the whole west end of the town seethed with the hysteria of the condemned, while a continual stream of offal poured down a gore-striped factory wall into the river. Lismore people seemed to raise a collective eyebrow at such phenomena, as much as to say, 'Is this the way for a town to conduct itself?' Nothing disturbed Lismore's peace and purity, nothing whatever.

But Cappoquin always seemed a free-and-easy place to me, maybe because it didn't have big buildings casting long shadows on it, and instead of slightly unreal street-names like Lismore's Fernville and South Mall had Pound Lane and Mill Street. The names on the shop-fronts were delightfully different too: Uniacke, Meskil, Gillespie, Herr .... And I loved the orphanage, it overlooked the hurling field. Sometimes marching down with the team I'd see the orphans being taken for a walk by the Sisters of Mercy who had charge of them, their mothers, as I thought then. I only remember that they were all boys, they were all dressed alike (grey jerseys, grey flannel trousers), and they all seemed the same size – the effect, no doubt, of having to walk two abreast in a rigid column. The sight of them provided me with a bracing dose of *schadenfreude*.

During those Sunday outings with the team, however, I saw more of the town's pubs than I did of the town itself. The pub was our home from home. Sometimes we plumped for Conway's Hotel, rather more rarely the Toby Jug (a true piece of Cappoquin novelty, that name, I thought), but mainly Jimmy Foley's 'The Railway Bar' was where we pitched camp. Jimmy was from Lismore, and a friend of Georgie's – they used to cycle competitively together. It struck me that Jimmy must have been the better of the two. Above the bar there was a colour photograph of someone on a real racing bike, in real racing kit – black shorts, wide-striped jersey, and a crash helmet that looked like a gorilla's mitten. Photos of Georgie were few and far between. And Jimmy had a prosperous air to him, he'd retired from competition, possibly even owned a car. Business was good, and he owned a greyhound, hoping no doubt that its phenomenal haunches would replicate – or maybe improve on – the thigh-power of his own sprightlier days.

It was in that small bar that each visit perfected itself, as I sat in a corner with a tumbler of the rust-coloured fizz that was called lemonade and a bag of dusty-tasting Marietta biscuits and, rapt, revelled in the company of men. Their playful jostling before the game, their nervous teasing, the rattle of coin and key as clothes were changed. The sleeveless singlets and cotton drawers, pale freckled shoulder-blades, the surprising sight of hairy legs. The few who had watches – Michael Madden, Ronnie O'Donnell – wrapped them up carefully in their hankies. Sonny Bransfield, home from England, leaning time after time on his angled stick to test its spring, hoping that this year, maybe, he'd rediscover the touch that he'd once been able to take for granted. A murmuring, a restlessness. Vacant, undirected whoops and shouts. Everybody hopeful, boyish, unrecognizably gay.

The game didn't matter. Lismore always lost. Tourin beat us, Tallow beat us, the Geraldines regularly hammered us, as did Affane and the Brickey Rangers. And when they first stumbled back into Jimmy's, team members often looked crestfallen or sheepish. But disappointment was amazingly short-lived, and Geo considered it bad form to denounce backsliders on the spot. In a twinkling there was hearty laughter and rounds of drinks, and soon – a true test of conviviality

– morbid ballads were aired. They sang, in ragged unison:

Goodbye Johnny dear and when you're far away
Don't forget your dear old mother far across the sea.
Write a letter now and then, and send her all you can.
And don't forget where'er you go that you're an Irishman.

After each song strong cries of approval went up – 'Good man,
Joe. Good man yourself!' – followed by a moment's silence
while an orchard of Adam's apples wobbled with draughts of
down-coursing porter. I sat amongst them with my mouth
open (its inside a kind of beach from biscuit crumbs and gassy
cordials), marvelling at all this ease and camaraderie, so rare,
yet seemingly so accessible, unable to do wee-wee even,
though I was bursting, the spell of my defeated, happy
townsmen was so strong.

3

'Are you awake, Seoirse?' Chrissy called softly.
Was I what? 'Awake' was hardly the word. Since the first
twitterings of dawn I'd been on full alert, charged to the hilt
with electric tension. This was the day of the big one. This was
the day for which those Cappoquin Sundays were a rehearsal.
Geo was taking me to Dublin for the All-Ireland.
I was sybaritically aware of what an extravagant treat it was
to attend the final of the national hurling championship and to
travel over a hundred miles in Corny Willoughby's Ford V8 in
order to do so. None of my pals had the ghost of a chance of
doing half as much. Most of them hadn't been to Dublin even
on an ordinary day. But there was just as much pleasure for me
in the thought that I was caught up in an event whose outcome
stirred the spirits of the vast majority of my fellow-country-
men, and that my heart would drum along with the pulse of
thousands and that my roar would contribute to the great roar.
I saw the event as an acting out of the old nationalist hymn 'A   143

Nation Once Again' (a temporary state, of course, but all the more precious and intense for that). And I hoped to feel more overwhelmingly and more delightfully than usual how good it was to have a self to cede to the collective.

Fuelling me further, everyone had high expectations of this particular clash. For weeks the newspapers had promised a 'classic encounter'. Would the purple-and-gold cohorts of Wexford come down 'like a wolf on the fold' on the stalwarths of Cork, the Rebel County?

In those days there wasn't a livelier question a national daily could ask. Economically, politically and every other way the country was dozing on the sideline, the national mood the inspiration of not much more than jokes. (The one about compilers of an Irish-Spanish dictionary having trouble translating *mañana* because nothing in Irish quite conveyed the same sense of urgency probably first surfaced in a Dublin pub *circa* 1952 or 1953.)

Yet in all the stagnation, hurling thrived, had its Golden Age indeed, or its Age of Ring as it should be called, since the chief igniter of interest and inspirer of purple prose was Christy Ring – superstar, genius and enemy (he played for Cork). For quick wits, speed over five to ten yards, instinct for undefended space, economy and wristiness of stroke, there never was anyone like him. He sprang into the country's torpid imagination like a flare in a fog. A damn shame, I thought, that he wasn't on our side. But at least I'd be seeing the great man. And then, think if we beat him?

As if anticipation of the game and sense of occasion weren't enough, and as though to ensure that I wouldn't be able to succumb completely to the collective, the day also promised a treat that would be all mine. (I wouldn't want it any other way, of course, but how wonderful when world collaborated with self!) I'd be seeing my Daddy at a totally unfamiliar time of the year, the first Sunday in September, when we were both in school. I'd bashfully drink in again the tanned face, the deep brown eyes, the jet-black hair swept back. I'd realize again – soon, soon! – with eye-opening, brimming confidence that I was his alone, he mine, the real thing, antecedent and superior to anything Lismore provided.

'Eat your breakfast, there,' said Mam, impatiently.

144   I couldn't. And every minute was an hour.

But soon we were off, stopping to pick up our last passenger, Billy Linneen, at the bridge (Geo and three or four of his pals had hired the car between them), then sliding smoothly up the mountain road, north towards Ireland.

Over the mountains with us, via the Vee, with the whole plain of Munster spread out beneath like a quilt of heaven, fertile Tipperary in green and gold, and in the shade of the Galtees the Golden Vale. On hummingly through Clogheen and Cahir, all fast asleep, and next Cashel of the Kings, with its massive, abbey-crowned rock, as isolated and lofty as the past itself, while opposite the ruin's main entrance sat the comprehensible present, the 'Rock' cinema.

The talk turned to why Tipperarymen were called 'stone-throwers', and a long and learned discussion ensued (we flew past the Horse and Jockey), featuring solemn references to Dan Breen and Sean Treacy, whose sons, it was plain, Geo and the other sojourners longed to be. We were beyond Urlingford, we were in Laois, a county nobody knew anything about, not even how to pronounce it. But there was the big jail in Portlaoise, and there was the castle in Portarlington where John McCormack lived.

'Count John.'

'I suppose he was called Count on account of all the money he made.'

'Yerra not at all,' disputatiously; 'Wasn't it the Pope made a Count of him?'

The car rocked with laughter, and to maintain the mood, someone sang a snatch of 'The Fairy Tree', breaking off when it came to the line, 'And Katie Ryan saw there' to ask, 'Is that one of them Ryans of Glenshask, I wonder?'

'The one with the crooked eyes?'

'I dunno is that all she has crooked?'

'Are you asking or telling, now?'

More explosions of laughter.

On we bowled, the increasing flatness of the land seeming to increase our speed, as though the openness made Dublin act like a magnet. We crossed the Curragh of Kildare – maledictions from a few, especially George, on the site of the political obscenity of their generation, the Curragh camp. Then the barracks at Newbridge and the wide main-street, then Naas and Mrs Lalor's fine old ivy-clad hotel. Almost 145 there. Billboards, double-decker buses, fast driving. Clondalkin, Walkinstown, Drimnagh – and, at last, tucked into that treeless vastness of public housing, Sundrive Road, where brick uniformity turned into uplift, landfall, hope.

There he was. 'Hello John,' said everyone, crowding around the front door, and I didn't get to say hardly anything, what with the throng, and feeling shy, and because the next thing we had to do was go to mass – short twelve, at St Bernadette's, Clogher Road – and then there was a lot of garbled big-people's talk about arrangements, Geo and his pals being in a terrible hurry to get a few pints in after the rigours of the road and before the minor game, but wanting to seem concerned about my day, as though my father's presence brought out the parent in all of them, until at last 'Up Wexford!' George called out the kitchen door to me, and they were gone.

I was in the garden, attempting to slip into my other life. That was the best place to reorient myself, to reintroduce myself to city birds (gulls and pigeons), to hear the nasal Dublin voices from the soccer game in the communal field beyond the garden wall, the voices of people Peg called 'gurriers'. I'd been rigorously instructed in Lismore that while the people who lived all around us – in Clogher Road, in Stanaway Road, and on up into Kimmage – were only recently converted slum-dwellers, Sundrive Road was somehow above all that, had to be, since it housed my father the school-teacher. But the raspy, glottal shouts from the field were a delight to me, conveying, I felt, the tang of the real Dublin, beckoning me away from my familiar self.

Perhaps it was a pity that I had no Dublin playmates, but I never bewailed their absence at the time. The city itself was my true friend. In it I found the measure of my yearning. Besides, the once or twice I talked with neighbouring kids they ended up asking me why I didn't live there all the time, obliging me to explain tearfully it was because my mother was dead. Then I'd run indoors, only for Daddy to greet me with an exasperated, 'Och, what is it now?' That made me cry even more, because I thought my tears had a truer basis than his prickliness, and because 'Och' was an Enniscorthy expression.

146   Still, I did think of the people next-door as my friends. A

mother and daughter (Mam and Chrissy figures, I suppose, but distanced and made bland by the change of bailiwick). They were just my kind of people. The girl (how is it that I can remember everything except their names?) worked in the Clarnico-Murray sweet factory, as she often generously reminded me. And better yet, they were related to Shay Elliott, the famous cyclist who rode in the Tour de France, a fact which delightfully connected me with a celebrity and connected them with my father, who knew all about the Tour. He'd been to France, after all, and not just Lourdes, either, but Rocamadour, where he had a pal, Maurice. And he told me about the race, the yellow jerseys, the national mania: it was like an All-Ireland that lasted two weeks. He could pronounce the names: Babet, Fausto Coppi. He could sing 'La Vie en Rose'. I was so proud of him.

I was alone in my pride, however.

Mam wrangled with him about money, about new clothes for me, about my tearful temperament ('that child can't bear correction'). As for Peggy, I chanced to find out how she felt during one of my summer visits. My father, unusually, had gone out for the evening, and I'd been sent to bed early because of the fuss I'd created at his going. I lay there snivelling, waiting for the pink, traffic-burdened evening to go away.

Downstairs, Peg must have thought I was asleep, or probably was unfamiliar with the acoustics of the house (never having been in my position and bred to the thick-walled silences of Swiss Cottage). In any case, out poured all her resentments, Mam encouraging her – Mam summered with Daddy and me until I was ten or so. My father didn't do a stroke around the house, he treated Peg like a skivvy, he'd never have a square meal if she didn't make it for him, he didn't care tuppence for his schoolwork ('and him with his BA and Higher Dip.Ed. A School Inspector he should be, not teaching in that slum in Inchicore'). And – horror of horrors! – he drank. Brendan Tiernan puked on the stairs. 'So I said to John, if you think I'm going to clean that up, you have your wax!' Peg's voice had a touch of a turkey-gobble in it and she relished afresh her indignation.

'You were right, girl,' said Mam, solemnly.

I heard it all, appalled. My father a boozer, no better than 147 any Church Lane clown. The tears came in earnest, then, a flood of anger and shame, as I lay wondering how I would lay up this picture of a life hitherto invisible in my store of specialness.

I've often tried since to reconstruct for myself the life I was denied in Sundrive Road. Judging by the house, it can't have amounted to much. At the time, of course, it was difficult for me to see that, or even to see the place simply as a house. It was a place tinged by the strangeness of my parents having briefly lived there. But, as a dwelling, it showed itself to be completely beyond the range of that golden moment.

Take the aborted front room. This was the most spacious room in the house, the one with the bay window, the one that most people I knew would make the home's centrepiece, complete with china cabinet, sofa and holy pictures. In the home I yearned for, the front room contained my father's bike, bundles and stacks of old papers and magazines, an upturned butter box rimmed with shoe-polish, and brushes, rags and tins on the floor around it. And dust. Layers – beaches – of it. An airless, neglected, rejected space; indifferently, negligently, knowingly accommodated, making a cipher of 'home', turning the house into an address, a depot. Domesticity's grave. My mother's memorial.

Only by lending the room emblematic force can its nullity be redeemed, and I'm all the more prompted to do that knowing now my father and I never did make a family. But as a know-nothing child, the room was just one strangeness among others, one of no great magnitude either. I used to visit it off and on, despite severe cautions not to ('You'll get your shirt all dirty'), and whiled away pleasant half-hours thumbing through old copies of *The Listener*, with its close-printed pages and sober livery. Once or twice, the room even provided a discovery. One was *Feasta*: the idea of anything written in Irish for grown-ups amazed me. Another discovery was of a tea-chest containing, among bits of bike gear and played-out Travelites, four old-fashioned notebooks, real good ones, with marbled board covers and stout spines and inside – incredibly – full of my father's hand-writing. My nervous skimming revealed the contents as the story of my father's youth. I put them aside guiltily. But the next time I looked for them, they and the tea-chest were gone.

148

I played at being bus conductor, running up and down stairs shouting 'Any more fares?' and standing at the closed front door intoning, 'Kelly's Corner', 'Dolphin's Barn', 'Step along now, please!' in my fake Dublin accent. A busman's life was the life for me. It was solitary, standing on the platform alone. It was citified: when my time to enrol came I intended to make it quite clear that I was prepared to man double-deckers only. And it combined to a nicety service and command.

When I was ordered to stop reciting my gazetteer of inner-city landmarks – a practice which I conceded might become tiresome, without quite seeing how – I went and pitted the wooden mantelpiece in the living-room with my father's tuning-fork, echoing its hum with a long, drawn-out one of my own, in imitation of Brother Blake trying to teach us to sing. Five minutes of this, however, and I was told, 'Oh, shut up.'

I liked being in the living-room, though. It wasn't dark. The bookshelves overflowed enticingly, sometimes disgorging treasures such as a picture book of Fernandel, whose title must have been *Forty Ways to Look Ovine and Happy*, or perhaps a photograph album with snaps of me when I wasn't the height of a bee's knee. There was a Bush radio, which, in contrast to the one in Lismore, looked like a real piece of cabinet-making, and which had a broad, sea-green dial, promising reception from Frankfurt, Hilversum and AFN. And there was a picture on the wall of a man in specs and a bow-tie.

'Who's that, Daddy?'

'W. B. Yeats.'

'Who's he?'

'A poet.'

'Oh.'

The Sunday of my All-Ireland excursion, I remember, Peg did not officiate at lunch, in fact she was nowhere to be seen. She must have decided that a load of countrymen pressing in, and for all she knew expecting to be fed as well, was more than she could face on her day off. I was disappointed, though, since I'd been hoping that maybe she'd have a bit of pork ready for me. (Pork was a great novelty. The butchers of Lismore didn't stock it. And it was in a meal of Peg's that I first 149 had it.) Peg's disinclination to serve us means, however, that I know exactly what I had for lunch that day. Bacon and cabbage, done in my father's inimitable way – the pressure cooker. This method, which I approved of on the grounds of speed and spectacle, invariably made the bacon awfully salty and reduced the cabbage to wraiths of singed steam.

I set-to with a will, however, and bolted down the meal in record time, partly to please Daddy – he disliked my finicky moods – and partly, of course, because we'd have to be getting a move on if we wanted to get to the game. Surprisingly, though, Daddy seemed in no hurry, lingering over the inevitable post-prandial cup of reddish-brown tea and drawing with relish on his John Player. Eventually, crushing the butt with exaggerated care, he said:

'Do you want to go to the match?'

Why yes of course, naturally, wasn't that what the whole day was about? What did he mean?

'Well,' he went on – 'It's a bit late now, and there'll be an awful crowd (so it'll be hard to see), and it looks like rain, so I thought we could go to the pictures, instead, if you like.'

'What's on?'

Half an hour later we were sitting in the Regal, I was scoffing a tub of HB ice-cream, and Kirk Douglas was warbling 'A Whale of a Tale'. *Twenty Thousand Leagues under the Sea*. And that was just about as far as I felt from the day's original promise.

I still don't know why I did it. Was it that I felt I had no option but to play along with whatever my father suggested, being so used to living in the shadow of his (and everybody else's) designs anyway? Was it, simply, that I just wanted to be with *him* more than anything else? Was it that I thought it smart to go to the cinema in the city, especially with a big noise from the Irish Film Society, which I believed Daddy to be.

When we were in town together (without Mam) he often took me up the three flights of tall stairs in North Earl Street to the Society's offices. I loved being able to look down on the pigeons and the roofs of double-deckers, while the names of Rossellini, De Sica and Ford ambled through the smoky air behind me. Mam attacked the whole thing as a waste of time, and said Daddy ought to be ashamed of himself for thinking more of a sideshow than of his teaching, advancing himself in his profession he should be – making more money. She never saw that the Society and its films provided most of the aesthetic pleasure and intellectual grist which my father needed in order to feel that he was living in the present, instead of in the limbo of widowerhood. So, in opting for the cinema, was I unconsciously siding with my father against Mam?

If I was, the impulse occurred at a depth of twenty thousand leagues in my psyche. The fact is, I had no sense of having deliberately done anything much at all until Geo and his mates came back, all flushed and glad-looking, and full of the game. It had been a classic, a thriller, worth going any length to see.

'A shame ye lost,' said Geo to me. That was the first I'd heard, or thought, of the result, but the news of it had no effect on me. Stimulated by my own day, I promptly blurted out, 'We didn't go. We went to the pictures.'

'The pictures!' Geo cried, and I knew then there was something wrong. 'Sure you could have done that in Lismore.'

A beam of pain irradiated a face slackened by porter and surprise.

I knew I'd betrayed him. Geo wasn't interested in me just then, however, but was glaring at my father. What was I to do now? I felt caught between them, in no-man's land.

But it was all right; we were leaving anyhow. Clumsily I threw my arms around my father and sidled out to the car. Evening was closing in. We glided away.

Soon, once the city had been forsaken, the men's talk picked up, the match was replayed blow by blow, and incident sparked memory. I listened lackadaisically, morosely. Not even the jolly stop at Mary Willy's – the half-way house – picked me up. The men let me be, imagining, no doubt, that I had Daddy on my mind. I had, of course. That tobaccoey smell, the rasp of that rough, dark cheek, that mellow voice made smooth by city usage. But what bore down on me much more heavily was the idea that I had inflicted on Georgie the worst injury of his hurling career. Just by doing nothing. Just because I was me. It was as though pain and conflict were endemic. Clash inevitable. And myself both agent and outcome. That's what I took with me down the long road home.